healthy eating during
chemotherapy

José van Mil with
Christine Archer-Mackenzie

healthy eating during
chemotherapy

For the first time, a chef and a medical specialist have
teamed up to inspire you with over 100 delicious recipes

Photography by Henk Brandsen
Kyle Books

An Hachette UK Company
www.hachette.co.uk

This edition published in 2018 by Kyle Books,
an imprint of Kyle Cathie Ltd
Carmelite House
50 Victoria Embankment
London EC4Y 0DZ
www.kylebooks.co.uk

ISBN 978 1 904 92088 5

Distributed in the US by Hachette Book Group,1290 Avenue of Americas,
4th and 5th Floors, New York, NY 10104

Distributed in Canada by Canadian Manda Group, 664 Annette St., Toronto,
Ontario, Canada M6S 2C8

Project Editor: Suzanna de Jong
Design: pinkstripedesign@hotmail.com
Copy Editor: Anna Hitchin
Americanizer: Delora Jones
Proofreader: Lesley Levene
Editorial Assistant: Vicki Murrell
Indexer: Alex Corrin
Photographer: Henk Brandsen
Home Economists: José van Mil, Hanneke Boers and Nadia Zerouali
Prop Stylist: Jan Willem van Riel
Production: Sha Huxtable

A Cataloguing in Publication record for this title is available from the British Library.

Printed and bound in China

10 9 8 7 6 5 4 3 2

contents

a world to thank

Having a dream is one thing, but to accomplish it, is quite a different matter. It's just like real life, you need the support, enthusiasm, encouragement, inspiration, and professional knowledge and feedback from others. And my goodness, what a beautiful bunch of people I have had to support me. Dr. Christine (Chrissie) Archer-Mackenzie, who has spent so much time and energy to provide a sound medical, nutritional, and cancer-related base. Marja Lantinga, dietitian at VUMC, who advised me on what patients can and won't eat and many other things related to food and cancer. Then inevitably, my husband, writer Paul Somberg, who unfortunately was both patient and at times 'ghost writer' and my dear friend Ruth Archer, who read, reread, and rereread again the manuscript and kept me sharp. As did Olga van Itallie, Carla van Mil, and Kantinka Paul.

Any book is a team effort. I may have written it, but this book is far more than words and recipes. The photo team did a magnificent job in picturing the dishes as attractively and realistically as possible. What a great job you made of it, Henk, Jan Willem, Hanneke, and Nadia; thank you ever so much for your professionalism and support.

All the recipes have obviously been tested extensively. Firstly in my trial kitchen (thank you Jasper & again Nadia) and then by many others who found themselves in difficulties with food-related problems due to their treatment. It was under these extremely difficult conditions that they crossed borders and tried the recipes. Thanks a lot Paul, Jorien (Ron's wife), Reina, and all the others, who —however ill—rewardingly confirmed that my approach to food for patients undergoing radiation and chemotherapy had an uplifting effect on them.

You can write a book, but getting it publicized is another matter. Thank you Kyle Cathie, Suzanne De Jong (my reliable and very professional guide), Anna Hitchin, Inmerc's John Voskens (who believed in the concept from the onset), Chris van Koppen (you're great), and last but not least, Frits Poiesz, a magnificent partner who straightened whatever ripples were left.

Finally, I owe a lot to my grandma "Oma Dien" who gave me the first insight in the value of certain foods when you're ill. She took me blackberry picking to make juice to help to cure my sister's measles. It worked.

you are my source of inspiration

To write this cookbook I have found my inspiration in my fantastic husband Paul, but also in Ian, Mignon, Ron, and all those others—patients and their supporters—whom all of a sudden find themselves confronted with food related problems due to chemo and radiation treatments.

To Paul and all these others I dedicate this book and hope they can find some joy and pleasure by eating and drinking well, and manage to keep up their strength.

José van Mil

introduction

a harsh reality

All of a sudden, I saw the light—there was something terribly wrong with my husband. Not just a common cold, not a backache, nor a spell of tiredness. No, it was something much more serious. The word sent shivers up my spine: cancer.

Immediate and radical medical treatments were required to bring things under control. Fortunately, the medical profession has come a long way in the treatment of cancer and the prospects for recovery are improving each year. In my husband's case, chemotherapy and radiotherapy were among the things in store for him. In order to successfully pass through this ordeal, it was crucial to make sure that he would not lose weight through malnourishment or lack of appetite. Normally, he loves his food but the effects of the treatment took their toll. Eating became a huge burden. And he was not alone in that. I talked to numerous cancer patients, their relatives, and friends, and almost all of them had encountered eating problems.

I therefore decided to make the most of my professional experience as a chef to develop a method to make eating easier for him. I contacted Christine Archer-Mackenzie and Marja Lantinga who improved my method and made valuable contributions from a professional medical and oncological dietitian's point of view. It worked wonderfully well, and during radiotherapy, intense chemotherapy, and stem-cell transplantation, my husband lost hardly any weight. Remarkably soon afterwards, he regained his strength and had fully recovered his appetite. Since then, other cancer patients have tried my method and it inspired most of them to keep eating. They also provided me with useful feedback.

Although I am not offering you a miracle cure with *Healthy Eating During Chemotherapy,* what this book can do is help cancer patients to keep eating and by doing so, aid their recovery from their treatment. It's definitely worth trying.

And through it all, be strong and keep up your spirits.
José van Mil

cancer and food

what is cancer?

Cells are constantly being replaced in the body. Each area of our body has a specialized function and specialized cells to perform that function. The way cells multiply is by dividing to create an exact replica with the same hereditary information (DNA). Normally, cell division is controlled so that a relatively constant size is maintained throughout adult life. Sometimes a fault can occur which causes cells to divide more rapidly than they should. A mechanism is in place to control this, but if this also fails, the cell replication rate of these "faulty" cells accelerates. The faulty cells absorb more nutrients and thus divide at an ever-increasing rate to form a tumor. If these cells do not leave their specific area, they are known as benign or non-cancerous cells. If the cells have the ability to invade neighboring tissue, they are then called cancer cells and produce cancerous tumors. When cancer cells invade other parts of the body, this is referred to as metastasis.

treatments for cancer

SURGERY
Surgery is the oldest form of treatment. It can be used both to diagnose and to treat cancer. It may be the sole treatment necessary or it may not be used at all, depending upon the site and the kind of cancer. Sometimes it is supplemented with other treatments, such as chemotherapy and radiotherapy.

CHEMOTHERAPY
Chemotherapy (and also radiotherapy) works by preventing cancer cells from multiplying. This is achieved by interfering with the cells' DNA so they are unable to replicate. The treatment can also cause some cancer cells to commit suicide. Chemotherapy involves having anti-cancer drugs administered into the bloodstream so that the whole body is affected. It's a powerful treatment that kills cancer cells and healthy cells alike. During chemotherapy, the body is not only fighting cancer but, at the same time, replacing healthy cells that are damaged by the chemotherapy drugs. Chemotherapy and radiotherapy particularly affect the cells lining the digestive tract, hair follicles, and bone marrow, resulting in problems with the mouth and throat, hair loss, anemia, bleeding, and an inability to fight infection.

SIDE EFFECTS
Common side effects during chemotherapy are changes in the sense of smell and taste, nausea, vomiting, mouth sores, anemia, changes in bowel habits, fatigue, pain, and weight loss. The general overall effect for patients is a combination of tiredness and lethargy, which in turn can lead to lack of appetite.

the importance of food

For people undergoing cancer treatment, food becomes very important. They require good nutritional support to maintain body weight and strength, to prevent body tissue from breaking down, to rebuild tissue, and to fight infection and fatigue. At the same time, the side effects of treatment often have a significant impact on the consumption of food and eating habits. They can affect the absorption, digestion, and the body's use of food, creating a health risk for cancer sufferers. Therefore, nutritional care is needed to maximize quality of life.

Scientific studies have now proved that good nutritional support helps the appetite, decreases the toxicity that is associated with treatment, and can alleviate side effects, all of which significantly improve patients' survival rates.

The idea that food is good for one's health is not new. More than 4,000 years ago, both the ancient Egyptians and the ancient Greeks used honey medicinally for burns, sores and wounds. Hippocrates (460–377 B.C.) believed in the benefits of good food—'Let food be thy medicine and medicine be thy food'—and emphasized the importance of using fresh plants and herbs in his diet.

WHY ARE CERTAIN FOODS SO IMPORTANT IN THE DIET OF CANCER PATIENTS?

In the 1990s, phytochemical compounds were discovered in fruit and vegetables. These are plant-specific compounds that protect the plants from disease, oxidation, insect infestation, and radiation. When we eat these compounds —called phytonutrients—they have a similar protective effect on our bodies. Phytonutrients can have anti-inflammatory, antibacterial, and anticancer properties in humans. The American National Cancer Institute is currently involved in research looking at the importance of these phytochemicals in cancer prevention and cancer treatments.

It will take scientists many more years before they know exactly how phytochemicals work. Below are some examples of foods containing phytonutrients that show promising results when it comes to fighting cancer.

ANTIOXIDANTS

To understand the importance of antioxidants, first we need to talk about free radicals. Oxygen is utilized by cells in our bodies—it is fundamental to our most basic mechanisms. Free radicals are the natural by-product of this oxidation process. These free radicals travel through cells, causing damage to the DNA and cell membranes. This damage can encourage the development of cancer in the cells.

Antioxidants work to prevent cells from becoming cancerous by enabling early cancer cells to become healthy cells again. Antioxidants can also prevent cancer by decreasing the levels of free radicals in our bodies.

You can compare the workings of free radicals and antioxidants with what happens to an avocado when you cut it open and expose the flesh. The avocado will turn brown due to oxidation which releases free radicals. If you squeeze some lemon juice over the avocado, this stops the browning, acting as an antioxidant.

A number of foods contain antioxidants with the potential to support cancer treatments. Their strength can vary enormously. Examples of antioxidants and foods containing high levels of antioxidants are:

Phenols – antioxidants found in berries, grapes, mustard, olive oil, sesame seeds, and tea

Selenium – a strong antioxidant that works best in combination with vitamin E, it's found in avocados, Brazil nuts, brewer's yeast, cereals, grains, shellfish, and sunflower seeds

Vitamin E – occurs in avocados, egg yolks, nuts, olive oil, seeds, tuna, and wheat germ

Beta carotene – found in brightly colored fruits and vegetables, especially those containing yellow pigment, this functions as an antioxidant that can prevent cancer; good sources are apricots, beets, broccoli, cantaloupes, carrots, cherries, peaches, peppers, pumpkins, spinach, squashes, and sweet potatoes

Vitamin C – noted for its high antioxidant activity, it has a protective effect on normal cells and a sensitizing effect on cancer cells; good sources are black currants, citrus fruits, parsley, rosehips, and all fruits and vegetables containing vitamin C.

Bioflavonoids – these pigments, found in fruits and vegetables, stop or slow the growth of cancer cells; good sources are apricots, lemons, and melons. Bioflavonoids and vitamin C are found in many of the same foods and seem to work together to have a positive effect on the immune system, which is very important when chemotherapy compromises the immune system. Foods that contain both vitamin C and bioflavonoids include the skins of grapes and the peel and pith of citrus fruits.

Also high in antioxidants and therefore helpful during chemotherapy are green tea, lycopene (found in cooked tomatoes), pomegranate juice, and artichokes, while curcumin (turmeric) acts as an antioxidant in normal cells and can cause cancer cells to die.

OTHER BENEFICIAL PHYTONUTRIENTS AND FOODS

Shiitake mushrooms contain a compound called **lentinan** which is believed to stop or slow tumor growth and have a positive effect on the immune system. Japanese researchers routinely give lentinan to patients undergoing chemotherapy for lung, nose, throat, and stomach cancers.

Current research suggests a potential benefit from the use of **phyto-estrogens**, especially in hormone-related cancers such as breast and prostate. They are effective in blocking cancer-promoting estrogens and they also reduce the toxic effect of chemotherapy and radiotherapy. Phyto-estrogens are found in linseed (flaxseed), rhubarb, and soy.

A substance called **IP6**, present in animal and plant cells, appears to inhibit the growth of cancer cells by changing the cells to make them become more normal. Raw vegetables, especially broccoli, cabbage, and cauliflower, and those high in dietary fiber, contain IP6 in abundance.

There is some evidence that **omega-3 fatty acids** may have specific benefits for cancer patients undergoing chemotherapy, reducing the growth of tumors. Omega-3

fatty acids, which are essential to human health, are not produced by the body and must therefore be obtained from food. They can be found in cold-water fish such as bass, cod, halibut, herring, mackerel, salmon, sardines, shark, and tuna. Omega-3 fatty acids can also be found in plants—they are then called alpha-linolenic acid (ALA). ALA can be found in flaxseed, kidney beans, and soybeans.

Foods high in **protein** are important because protein helps build and repair tissue, retain muscle mass, and also maintain a healthy immune system. Following surgery and during cancer treatment, additional protein is usually needed to heal tissue and help prevent infection. The best choices to meet protein needs are foods that are low in saturated fat. Good sources are eggs, fish, lean meat, podded plants (beans, peas, etc.) nonfat and lowfat dairy products, nuts, poultry, dried legumes, seeds, and soy products.

Research has confirmed that **honey** has healing properties. It can kill bacteria and is helpful in supporting the immune system. The sweet recipes in this book use honey rather than sugar where possible.

what to avoid

Try to eliminate processed, refined foods and stick to fresh, organic ingredients, if possible. Read all labels carefully to make sure that food contains no chemical additives. Freshly cooked ham is one thing; supermarket ham in a package with preservatives is another. Refined sugar and sweeteners such as aspartame, which, in the UK, is frequently found in yogurts, cereals, and already-prepared meals, have been linked to a range of diseases including cancer and are best avoided.

advice for specific cancer types

Always consult your specialist and oncology dietitian about what you should and shouldn't eat with your type of cancer.

Patients with **head and neck cancers**, including esophageal and gastric cancers, invariably need extra nutritional support. A dry mouth is often seen and requires soft or very moist foods. Some patients prefer strong-flavored foods. Tart foods can help increase the production of saliva. However, acidic or spicy foods are often not well tolerated. Ice-cold grapes and melon, eaten right from the fridge in small quantities, make great snacks.

Patients with **upper gastro-intestinal cancer** run the risk of malnutrition due to chronic bowel discomfort resulting in diarrhea and irritable bowels. Dried beans, dried fruit, fiber cereals, milk and milk products, nuts, popcorn, seeds, and corn are best avoided. Eat low-residue, low-fiber foods such as applesauce, bananas, rice, and toast. Avoid dehydration by drinking as much as you can, starting with sips and increasing the volume until you stop feeling uncomfortable. Dehydration salts may help.

Patients with **prostate and breast cancers**, both hormone-related cancers, may benefit from a milk- and dairy-free diet. Some people think that the hormones meant for the benefit of young calves, which are often present in dairy products, are the culprit. Certainly in China, where people eat a predominantly dairy-free diet, very few prostate and breast cancers are observed. Patients with these cancers may want to reduce their intake of milk by using currently available alternatives, such as coconut, oat, rice, and soy milk.

dietary supplements

Scientific evidence for the use of dietary supplements is currently inconclusive. Some cancer experts advise against taking supplements with antioxidant activity during treatment, claiming they could counteract the effectiveness of the chemotherapy. According to these scientists, antioxidants present in food should provide all the patient needs. However, other researchers believe that there may be benefits in taking supplementary antioxidants, to help protect normal cells from the damage the chemotherapy causes. When treatment has finished, some practitioners recommend supplements. Always check with your oncologist.

what's the problem?

Once a person has been diagnosed with cancer, chemotherapy may be offered as a treatment, but it will nearly always bring with it some less than pleasant side effects. One that will have a profound impact on one's daily life is the marked change in one's appreciation of food. Not only the cancer itself but also the side effects of treatment will affect one's eating habits.

Different types of cancer have different effects on eating. Nausea, vomiting and diarrhoea are a particular problem; many people lose weight through malnourishment because they cannot keep their food down. As a result, they get weaker and their recovery is adversely affected. If a specific cancer affects the mouth, throat, or digestive system, it is likely to significantly reduce the appetite, too.

The side effects of chemotherapy and radiotherapy are bound to have a major impact as well. The mouth can become dry as production of saliva diminishes. Mucus membranes can be badly affected, making swallowing difficult and sometimes painful. Blisters can make the mouth and throat dry and sore, affecting the way the mouth feels, and certain types of medication will cause constipation. In other words, the patient will be presented with a set of circumstances that makes the thought of eating unattractive and at times even repulsive.

all your senses are in disarray

On top of that, the tastes that are so familiar with—sweet, sour, bitter, salty—will seem to have changed. Instead of the sensations and experiences one is used to, completely new ones manifest themselves, and very often they are not agreeable. Favorite dishes, snacks, and even fruit may taste awful all of a sudden. Normal tap water may acquire an acidic taste and spicy flavors may be transformed into something profoundly bitter. For some patients, orange juice, which is known to be very healthy, seems to burn its way down their throat into the stomach.

Other senses may be affected as well. The smell of food can be very disturbing and may cause nausea or vomiting. Often the sight of a big plate of food, or watching others enjoying plates heaped with food, can put the patient off completely.

It is not only the physical difficulties that make mealtimes a challenge; there is also a psychological dimension. After the diagnosis, the patient may feel threatened, confused and afraid, rebellious, or completely shocked and in denial. So eating easily becomes an issue: something that's difficult and painful to do and that adds more fear and confusion to an already deeply unpleasant situation.

making the best of a difficult situation

Meals have acquired a wider social function in our society. Breakfast, lunch, and dinner are times to exchange feelings and the experiences of the day, and are important for everyone involved. When one of those people is being treated for cancer, the menu requires careful consideration. Whoever is cooking needs to be aware of the kinds of food the patient can have and may feel like eating—this can vary from treatment to treatment and from day to day. In most cases, it's a matter of finding the right texture and temperature, along with determining whether they'd prefer savory or sweet. In other words, it's a question of trial and error to discover what suits the patient best.

Their eating patterns will be unpredictable. Many patients feel embarrassed and worry about letting the cook down by eating just a mouthful. They may not even be able to eat at all, or may change their minds and prefer something else. Normal mealtimes no longer apply, and they'll eat what they can, when they can. The good news is that most side effects disappear shortly after finishing the treatment.

the aims of this book are:

1 To stimulate patients undergoing chemotherapy and radiotherapy to eat what they can when they can, in order to prevent weight loss and to keep up their strength as much as possible.

2 To ensure that the ingredients used in cooking for those undergoing chemotherapy and radiotherapy are beneficial to the patient.

3 To provide support, encouragement, and inspiration to those cooking for someone undergoing cancer treatment.

4 To help the patient to enjoy their food and drink as much as possible within the limits of the treatment.

the method

This is a book with a mission. It aims to help patients and carers overcome—as best as possible—the various eating problems commonly associated with chemotherapy and radiotherapy: a painful mouth, a dry throat, a sensitive digestive system, difficulty in swallowing, loss of appetite, and nausea. During treatment, the intensity of these problems will vary with the effect of the chemicals and radiation on the body and on the mind.

The method devised involves structuring each chapter in such a way that it follows the preferences of most cancer patients when it comes to choosing what to eat. By adhering to this structure, patients and carers can easily pick the dishes that are best suited to patients' likes and needs, thus increasing the chance that they will actually want to eat the food prepared for them. They may even enjoy it!

texture

During and after treatment, a patient's sense of taste and smell will be unreliable. To increase the likelihood of patients eating food—any food—carers need to focus on the food's texture and temperature, rather than on ingredients. Therefore, the chapters in this book are divided into six textures, each offering healthy, nourishing dishes.

LIGHT
The dishes in this chapter are characterized by their fluffy, soft texture. When eating a Light recipe, it isn't necessary to chew, so even patients with a sore mouth or throat can eat them.

SMOOTH
With their creamy texture, the dishes in this chapter will slip down easily when chewing and even swallowing are difficult as a result of an extremely dry, sore mouth and throat.

SOFT WITH A BITE
These dishes can be eaten when chewing isn't the biggest problem and the mouth and throat are not too sore. Even for patients with a fairly dry mouth, most of them are easy to cope with.

LIQUID
For patients with a badly affected mouth and throat who find chewing and swallowing painful, liquid "foods" like the dishes in this chapter are a suitable option.

CRISPY
Crispness has a great influence on the appetite—it might just persuade people who have no craving for food whatsoever to take a bite. Crispy food will only work when mouth and throat are not sore, painful, or dry, and when chewing and swallowing are not a problem.

FIRM
These dishes bring back a semblance of everyday food, but the portions remain small so they don't overwhelm patients by their sheer bulk. They are suitable when the throat and mouth are not too affected, and chewing and swallowing are possible.

temperature

After texture, patients are most likely to prefer a certain temperature—cold or warm. Every chapter therefore moves from a selection of cold dishes (both savory and sweet) to warm dishes (also savory and sweet).

The sweet dishes aren't desserts as such but "meals" in their own right, just like the savory dishes. Remember, it's what patients can eat and want to eat that's important; if that means eating sweet dishes only, so be it. This explains why you'll find sweet dishes scattered throughout the chapters rather than at the back of each chapter, as you might expect in a traditional cookbook.

flavor

Finally, every chapter offers a selection of mild dishes as well as dishes that are stronger-tasting, to cater for a wide range of patients, from those who have become very sensitive to flavors, to those whose sense of taste has diminished.

The arrangement of the recipes in each chapter is therefore:

- ❥ cool and savory with a mild flavor
  - ❥ cool and savory with a strong flavor
    - ❥ cool and sweet
      - ❥ warm and savory with a mild flavor
        - ❥ warm and savory with a strong flavor
          - ❥ warm and sweet

portion size

Many cancer patients undergoing chemotherapy and radiotherapy feel intimidated when large amounts of food are placed in front of them. Because their sensory system is completely off balance, a loaded plate represents an avalanche of smells, flavors, and colors that is often threatening and can cause a complete mental block against food.

It is much easier for patients to eat small meals at various times of the day. You will find that the recipes in this book all make two or three small portions. By eating together, patients and carers will have the opportunity to share an important part of their day and this may bring back some of the enjoyment of food. Although freshly prepared food offers the best nutritional value, it is possible to keep most dishes for a day or two in the fridge or to freeze them.

hygiene

People undergoing invasive treatments have a compromised immune system. Anyone cooking for them needs to be particularly aware of food hygiene, making sure all fruit and vegetables, tools, cutting boards, cutlery, and plates are cleaned thoroughly. Dishtowels and dishcloths must be changed after every use and washed on a high temperature.

about the recipes

The recipes in this book have been developed for cancer patients of (almost) all ages: youngsters (but not babies or small children), adolescents, adults, and the elderly.

In most cases, if you want to stimulate patients to eat, the trick is to find foods with the right texture and temperature for them and establish a preference for savory or sweet.

Recipes have been kept as simple and inspiring as possible, focusing on fresh, healthy ingredients. Other members of the family might easily be tempted to join in. To allow for this, each recipe also gives the ingredients needed to feed a family of four, including the patient.

The ultimate aim is clear: to ensure the intake of as much essential food as possible under the circumstances. Always remember, eating anything is better than nothing!

will it work?

The method described in this book will not work for everybody—each patient is different, circumstances vary, and not everybody reacts to cancer therapies in a predictable way. That said, it will help in identifying dishes that are as suitable as possible for individual patients. However, in situations when no food can be eaten at all, malnourishment becomes a serious risk. In that case, supplements and even stomach tube feeding must be considered.

the good foods list

Highly recommended (buy organic, if possible)

Apricots
Artichokes
Asparagus
Avocados
Bananas
Beans
Beets
Berries
Black currants
Brazil nuts
Brewer's yeast
Broccoli
Cabbage
Carrots
Cauliflower
Cereals
Cherries
Citrus fruits, including zest
  (except grapefruit)
Cod
Cranberries
Eggs
Fish
Flaxseed oil (Linseed oil)
Game
Garlic

Ginger
Grains
Grapes
Halibut
Herring
Kiwi fruit
Lean meat
Leeks
Legumes
Mackerel
Melons
Nuts
Oily fish
Olive oil
Onions
Parsley
Peaches
Peppers
Pomegranate juice
Poultry
Pumpkin
Rhubarb
Rosehip
Salmon
Sardines
Sea bass (e.g., grouper)

Seeds
Sesame seeds
Shark
Shellfish
Shiitake mushrooms
Soy products
Spinach
Spirulina (available
  in health shops)
Squash
Sunflower seeds
Sweet potatoes
Tea: green and white,
  herbal teas, rooibos
Tomatoes
Tuna
Turmeric
Vegetables
Wheat germ

Use occasionally

Butter

Coffee

Dairy products: non-
and low-fat are best
(none for patients with
breast and prostate
cancers)

Deep-fried foods (fried
only in extra virgin
olive oil at the right
temperature)

Honey

Pâté

Red meat

Red wine

Salt, kosher salt,
and sea salt

Saturated fats

Scotch (only good
malt whisky)

Smoked foods

Sugar

Avoid

Alcohol (most types,
except red wine and
good malt Scotch
whisky)

Barbecued
or burnt foods

Cookies (unless
homemade with
good ingredients)

Cakes (unless
homemade with
good ingredients)

Doughnuts

Fast foods

Soft drinks
(carbonated)

Grapefruit

Margarine:
hydrogenated or
partly hydrogenated

Processed foods, e.g.,
cheese, sausages,
hot dogs, ham

Sweeteners

White bread

White refined flour

hints and tips

eating and drinking

❧ Appetite is likely to fluctuate wildly, so embrace any occasion when patients want to eat, even if it's the middle of the night!

❧ Some people will eat better at certain times of the day, so try to find out the optimum times for them.

❧ The sight of big portions can be nauseating, so small portions are recommended—and not just for patients, but for those eating with them, too. If a patient's appetite increases, you can always enlarge the portions (simply multiply the quantities by two or three), or serve seconds.

❧ To make their food taste better, patients can try rinsing their mouth with water before eating, or brushing their tongue lightly with a wet toothbrush.

❧ Have them try to eat slowly and chew well to help digestion.

❧ It is important for them to keep the body's fluid level up, so ensure they keep sipping water or green tea, whatever their symptoms. Have them try to avoid drinking at the same time as eating.

❧ If they suffer from nausea or vomiting, avoid allowing cooking smells to enter their eating area. Have them wear comfortable, loose-fitting clothes and tell them to keep their head upright after eating.

❧ Conventional knives and forks may leave an unpleasant, metallic taste in the mouth. Using plastic knives and forks is a good solution.

❧ Anesthetic sprays are now available for patients to use in the mouth and throat to enable them to eat more easily.

❧ Keep healthy snacks close at hand for nibbling when required. Snack ideas are scattered throughout the book.

in hospital

❧ Eat a very light meal before your treatment, or take a snack with you to eat while traveling to the hospital if the journey is long.

❧ It is recommended that you drink water both before and during chemotherapy. Keep this up for a couple of days after treatment to flush the chemicals through. Aim to drink between eight and ten glasses per day. Green tea is also excellent.

❧ Avoid eating right after treatment for a few hours.

choosing the right dish

❧ Finding which foods suit patients best will be a case of trial and error. Using the method recommended by this book, focusing on texture first, then temperature and flavors, can be the key to success.

❧ Experience with cancer patients has shown that there's often an initial preference for a sweetish taste, even in non-sweet dishes. Many recipes in this book therefore have a sweet element to them.

❧ Smell and presentation are two other important factors that influence the appreciation of food. Try to find out what appeals and equally what repels.

❧ Whenever you sense an appreciation for certain tastes or textures, try to expand on these.

❧ The type of food that achieves the best results during treatment is often very difficult to pinpoint and may change over time. Keep on trying and always be flexible.

❧ Whenever possible, choose ingredients that are considered beneficial to cancer patients in general and to the type of cancer concerned in particular. The Good Foods List (see page 20) can help.

❧ Try to avoid the foods that are advised against (see pages 12 and 21) if you can. However, sometimes you will have to compromise—it's better for the patient to be eating something rather than nothing. If necessary, sparingly use non-recommended ingredients like fructose or even sugar—they could prove to be the irresistible ingredient that makes a recipe work.

❧ Tart foods are often pleasing to those with dry mouths —they stimulate the production of saliva.

❧ If eating of drinking dairy products results in heightened mucus production, you'd better choose savory dishes using dairy products as the salt in savory foods has a clearing effect on the mucus.

❧ If you suffer from nausea and vomiting, bland foods and mild flavors are often wise choices. Eating dry foods first thing in the morning may help. Ginger can also be effective in controlling nausea—try ginger ale, ginger tea, or gingersnaps.

❧ When the sense of taste has all but disappeared, try seasoning dishes more strongly than usual, or choose a strong-flavored recipe from this book, in order to provide some sort of taste distinction.

❧ Gas, bloating, and cramping can be helped by eating little and often, and avoiding carbonated drinks and drinking through a straw.

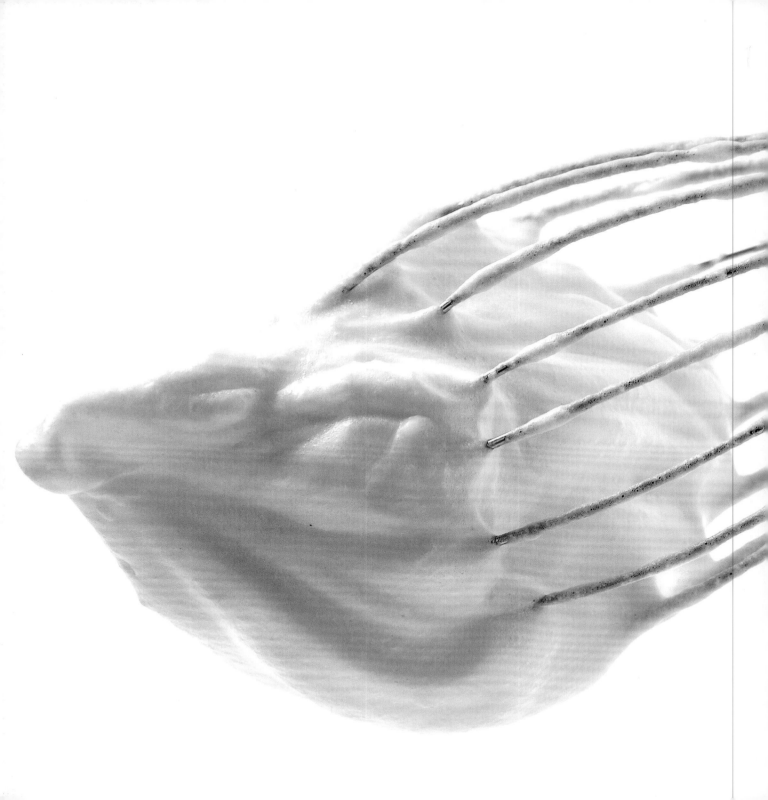

chapter one

light

carrot cream

This puree can also be made with pumpkin, beets, cauliflower, or broccoli instead of carrots. For a change, try adding a little chopped fresh ginger and replacing the honey with ginger syrup. For more flavor, turmeric or curry powder may be added to taste.

5 small carrots
1 small onion
1 garlic clove
1 orange
1/2 slice wholewheat bread
3 sprigs of fresh parsley
splash of olive oil

honey
pinch of salt
pinch of pepper
1/4 cup live-cultured yogurt
  or soy

2 small portions

Peel and chop the carrots. Peel and chop the onion and garlic. Wash the orange, grate the zest, and squeeze out the juice. Remove the bread crusts and cut the bread into small cubes. Finely chop the parsley.

Heat the splash of olive oil in a saucepan. Add the carrots, onion, garlic, and orange zest, and fry for 3 minutes over a medium heat. Add the bread cubes, orange juice, and just enough water to cover the carrots. Cook until the carrots are very soft, 10–15 minutes.

Whizz in a blender or food processor to a smooth puree. Add 1/2–1 teaspoon honey, the salt and pepper to taste, and set aside to cool.

Whisk the yogurt and carrot puree together. Add three-quarters of the parsley, adjust the seasoning to taste, and whisk for a few minutes more.

Spoon into small bowls or glasses and sprinkle with the rest of the parsley.

FOR A FAMILY OF FOUR:
MULTIPLY THE INGREDIENTS BY SIX AND SERVE AS AN APPETIZER
OR AS A SIDE DISH WITH FISH OR POULTRY.

beet and goat cheese whip

Good balsamic vinegar is slightly sweet and soft at the same time. It goes very well with beets but can be replaced by any other vinegar. If you choose to do this, add some extra honey to get a nice sweet and sour balance.

sprig of fresh parsley
1 small cooked beetroot
1/2 cup fresh goat cheese
   or soy yogurt
1/2–1 teaspoon honey
1/2 tablespoon balsamic vinegar
salt and pepper

2 small portions

Chop the parsley very finely.

Whizz the beet in a blender or food processor. Ensure the puree is as fine as possible. Add all the other ingredients except the parsley and whizz for a few more minutes until the mixture is light and fluffy. Add salt and pepper to taste.

Spoon into small bowls or glasses and sprinkle with the parsley.

Tip: This recipe can also be made with cooked carrots, pumpkin, zucchini, or eggplant.

FOR A FAMILY OF FOUR:
MULTIPLY THE INGREDIENTS BY FOUR AND SERVE AS AN APPETIZER.

fluffy tomato cream

This cream is finished off by sprinkling some chopped chives on top. The chives can also be mixed into the cream, and celery leaf or dill can be used instead of chives.

2 stems of fresh chives
1/2 cup whipping cream or soy cream
2 tablespoons live-cultured or soy yogurt
2/3 cup tomato puree
pinch of salt
pinch of pepper
pinch of curry powder

2 small portions

Chop the chives very finely.

Whip the cream with the yogurt, tomato puree, a pinch of salt, a pinch of pepper, and a pinch of curry powder until creamy and fluffy.

Divide the cream between two small glasses and sprinkle the chives on top.

Tip: Curry powder is optional. It contains turmeric, so you can use just turmeric instead of curry powder if you prefer.

FOR A FAMILY OF FOUR:
MULTIPLY THE INGREDIENTS BY FOUR AND SERVE AS AN APPETIZER.

snacks

Some recommended ready-to-eat light and soft snacks are pâtés, and fish mousses, such as salmon, and sweet mousses. When buying ready-made snacks, try and go for ones without preservatives and preferably without hydrogenated fats. Try to buy organic products if at all possible.

smoked chicken and almond mousse

This dish can be prepared in advance, but it is better to whip and add the cream just before serving.

about 1/3 cup smoked chicken
2 tablespoons ground almonds
1/2 tablespoon mayonnaise
1/2 tablespoon tomato ketchup
salt and pepper
1/3 cup whipping cream or soy cream

2 small portions

Whizz the chicken and ground almonds together in a blender or food processor. Make sure that the mixture is as fine as possible. Transfer to a bowl and stir in the mayonnaise and ketchup. Add salt and pepper to taste.

Whip the cream until fluffy and fold it into the chicken mixture.

Divide the mousse between two small dishes.

Tip: Soy cream will not get as stiff as whipping cream. It may be replaced by live-cultured or soy yogurt. However, then the mousse will not be as fluffy.

FOR A FAMILY OF FOUR:
MULTIPLY THE INGREDIENTS BY FOUR AND SERVE AS AN APPETIZER.

whipped tuna with orange

For the right texture, the tuna and orange mixture should be whizzed until very fine. If necessary, put it through a strainer or food mill before serving. Instead of tuna, cooked or canned salmon, or cooked shrimp can be used.

1/4 cup cooked or canned tuna
1/4 cup fresh orange juice
1/2 tablespoon mayonnaise
1 tablespoon live-cultured or soy yogurt
1/3 cup whipping cream or soy cream
pinch of salt
pinch of pepper

2 small portions

Whizz the tuna and orange juice together in a blender or food processor. Make sure the mixture is as fine as possible. Add the other ingredients and whizz for a few more minutes until the mixture is light and fluffy.

Divide the mousse between two glasses.

Tip: Since orange zest is considered to be healthy and is also very tasty, you may want to add some to this dish.

FOR A FAMILY OF FOUR:
MULTIPLY THE INGREDIENTS BY FOUR
AND SERVE AS AN APPETIZER.

light blueberry yogurt cream

Other berries or soft fruit may be used instead of fresh blueberries. This recipe also works well with frozen fruit, though you must defrost the fruit first. Instead of honey, a 100% fruit jam (with no added sugar) may be used to sweeten the cream.

$3/4$ cup blueberries
$2/3$ cup live-cultured or soy yogurt
$1/2$–1 tablespoon honey
$1/3$ cup whipping cream or soy cream

2 small portions

Wash the blueberries thoroughly and pat them dry with some kitchen paper.

Whizz the blueberries in a blender or food processor. Ensure the puree is as fine as possible. Add the yogurt and honey to taste, and whizz for a minute longer.

Whip the cream in a big bowl. (Soya cream will not get as stiff as whipping cream.) Add the blueberry mixture and fold it into the cream.

Divide the cream between two glasses.

FOR A FAMILY OF FOUR:
MULTIPLY THE RECIPE BY FOUR AND SERVE AS A DESSERT.

cream of fig and banana

To prevent the banana from discoloring, you can sprinkle it with some lemon juice. If you do, add a tiny bit of extra honey to make sure the cream is sweet enough.

2 dried figs
1/2 banana
2/3 cup live-cultured or soy yogurt
1/2–1 teaspoon honey
1/3 cup whipping cream or soy cream

2 small portions

Cut off the hard "stem" of the figs and peel the banana.

Whizz the figs and banana in a blender or food processor to a very fine puree. Add the yogurt and the honey and whizz for another minute.

Whip the cream in a big bowl. (Soya cream will not get as stiff as whipping cream.) Add the banana mixture and fold it into the cream.

Divide the cream between two small bowls or glasses.

Tip: The dried figs may be replaced by dates or prunes.

FOR A FAMILY OF FOUR:
MULTIPLY THE INGREDIENTS BY FOUR AND SERVE AS A DESSERT.

apple and cinnamon whip

It is easiest to use applesauce from a jar for this recipe. If you want to make fresh applesauce, sweeten it with honey rather than sugar.

¹/₂ cup applesauce
3 scoops soft vanilla ice cream
¹/₂ teaspoon ground cinnamon

2 small portions

Whizz all the ingredients together in a blender or food processor until smooth and fluffy.

Divide between two glasses.

Tip: Applesauce may be replaced by apricot compote.

FOR A FAMILY OF FOUR:
MULTIPLY THE INGREDIENTS BY THREE AND SERVE AS A DESSERT.

raspberry mousse

This mousse is quite soft and can be drunk through a thick straw. If raspberry seeds are going to be a problem, you may want to strain the puree through a fine mesh strainer before folding it in with the whipped cream.

4 ounces raspberries (about ³/₄–1 cup)
scant ¹/₂ cup ready-made custard
1 teaspoon honey
¹/₃ cup whipping cream or soy cream

2 small portions

Wash the raspberries carefully and pat them dry with some paper towels.

Whizz the raspberries in a blender or food processor. Ensure the puree is as fine as possible. Add the custard and honey and whizz for another minute.

Whip the cream in a big bowl. Add the raspberry mixture and fold it into the cream.

Divide the mousse between two small bowls or glasses.

Tip: Soy cream will not whip as stiff as whipping cream. It may be replaced by live-cultured or soy yogurt, in which case the mousse will not be quite as fluffy.

FOR A FAMILY OF FOUR:
MULTIPLY THE INGREDIENTS BY FOUR AND SERVE AS A DESSERT.

turkey, walnut, and spinach mousse

In this recipe the mousse is prepared with fresh spinach. You could use about an ounce of frozen spinach instead—add it to the turkey and heat until it is defrosted and hot.

about 1/4 cup turkey fillet
splash of olive oil
pinch of salt
pinch of pepper
about 2 ounces fresh spinach
1 egg
2 tablespoons shelled walnuts
1 slice wholewheat bread
2 tablespoons crème fraîche
    or soy cream

2–3 small portions

Preheat the oven to 350°F.

Cut the turkey into small pieces.

Heat a splash of olive oil in a big frying pan. Add the turkey, a pinch of salt and pepper, and fry for 5 minutes. Add the spinach and stir-fry for 3 minutes.

Separate the egg.

Whizz the walnuts in a blender or food processor until very fine. Add the bread and whizz to make breadcrumbs. Add the turkey mixture, crème fraîche, and egg yolk. Whizz to a smooth cream.

Beat the egg white with a pinch of salt until stiff. Fold into the turkey mixture. Divide the mixture between two or three small greased oven dishes, such as ramekins, and bake in the oven for 15 minutes until just set.

Serve hot.

Tip: The crème fraîche can be replaced by fresh goat cheese.

FOR A FAMILY OF FOUR:
MULTIPLY THE RECIPE BY THREE AND SERVE AS AN APPETIZER.

the benefits of olive oil

In cold dishes, use flaxseed oil or olive oil, since they are the best for your digestive system. In hot dishes, use only extra virgin olive oil since it is considered to be the best for your health.

eggplant and herb mousse

This mousse can be enjoyed both hot and cold, and it can also be used as a dip for vegetables and bread.

1 scallion
1/4 eggplant
splash of olive oil
pinch of salt
pinch of pepper
1 egg
1/2 slice wholewheat bread

sprig of fresh parsley
stem of fresh chives
sprig of fresh dill
1 plum tomato (canned)

2 small portions

Wash and chop the scallion. Wash the eggplant and cut into pieces.

Heat the olive oil in a big frying pan, add the scallion, and fry for 2 minutes over a medium heat. Add the eggplant and fry for 5 minutes over a low heat. Add the salt and pepper.

Separate the egg.

Whizz the bread and herbs in a blender or food processor to make herbed breadcrumbs. Add the tomato, eggplant mixture, and egg yolk, and whizz to a very fine, smooth cream.

Put the mixture in a double boiler (or simply a bowl) over simmering water and cook, stirring constantly, for about 5 minutes. Season to taste.

Beat the egg white until stiff. Fold into the eggplant mixture and cook for a few more minutes.

Divide between two small dishes and serve immediately.

Tip: As an additional fresh touch, you can serve this mousse with some live-cultured or soy yogurt on the side.

FOR A FAMILY OF FOUR:
MULTIPLY THE INGREDIENTS BY THREE, BUT USE A WHOLE SMALL EGGPLANT.
SERVE AS AN APPETIZER OR SIDE DISH.

steamed chicken, apricot, and curry mousse

Try smoked chicken or cooked ham instead of fresh chicken. Turmeric can also be added if you like.

1 small onion
about 1/4 cup chicken fillet
2 ready-to-eat dried apricots
splash of olive oil
pinch of salt
pinch of pepper
pinch of curry powder
1 egg
1/2 slice wholewheat bread

2 small portions

Peel and chop the onion. Cut the chicken and apricots into small pieces.

Heat a splash of olive oil in a frying pan, add the onion, and fry for 3 minutes over a medium heat. Add the chicken, a pinch of salt, a pinch of pepper, and a pinch of curry powder. Fry for another 5 minutes.

Separate the egg.

Whizz the bread in a blender or food processor to make breadcrumbs. Add the chicken mixture, apricots, and egg yolk, and whizz to a smooth cream.

Beat the egg white with a pinch of salt until stiff. Fold into the chicken mixture.

Divide the mixture between two small greased heatproof dishes such as ramekins. Cover the dishes with foil, place in the top of a steamer pan over boiling water and cover the pan. Steam for about 10 minutes until just set.

Place the dishes on small plates and serve warm.

Tip: It is strongly recommended that you use wholewheat bread, even though it makes the mousse a bit less light. You can use white bread, but it is not as healthy.

FOR A FAMILY OF FOUR:
MULTIPLY THE RECIPE BY FOUR AND SERVE AS AN APPETIZER.

creamy fish soufflé

Unlike white fish, mackerel contains essential fatty acids. For a change you could also try other fatty fish, such as trout, salmon, or tuna.

2 eggs
½ slice wholewheat bread
3 sprigs of fresh parsley
3-ounce fillet steamed or
   smoked mackerel
1 grilled red pepper from a jar
salt and pepper

2 small portions

Preheat the oven to 425°F.

Separate the eggs.

Whizz the bread and parsley in a blender or food processor to make herbed breadcrumbs. Add the mackerel, red pepper, and egg yolks, and whizz to a smooth cream. Season to taste.

Beat the egg whites with a pinch of salt until stiff. Fold into the fish mixture.

Divide the mixture between two small greased oven dishes, such as ramekins, and bake in the oven for 15 minutes until just set.

Serve immediately.

Tip: You could use a fresh red pepper and broil it yourself, but make sure it doesn't blacken when it's in the oven. Put it in a plastic bag when soft. Close the bag and let the pepper cool. Skin, cut in pieces and mix them with a dash of vinegar and a few drops of honey.

FOR A FAMILY OF FOUR:
MULTIPLY THE INGREDIENTS BY THREE AND SERVE AS AN APPETIZER.

mushroom mousse

This is like a soufflé and is baked in the oven. It can also be steamed or prepared in a double boiler.

6 ounces mushrooms
1 small onion
1 garlic clove
splash of olive oil

1 egg
1 thin slice wholewheat bread
salt and pepper

2 small portions

Preheat the oven to 350°F.

Wipe the mushrooms clean and chop them. Peel and chop the onion and garlic.

Heat a splash of olive oil in a big frying pan, add the onion, and fry for 3 minutes over a medium heat. Add the garlic and mushrooms and fry for another 5 minutes.

Separate the egg.

Whizz the bread in a blender or food processor to make breadcrumbs. Add the mushroom mixture and the egg yolk and whizz to a smooth cream. Add salt and pepper to taste.

Beat the egg white with a pinch of salt until stiff. Fold into the mushroom mixture.

Divide the mixture between two small greased oven dishes, such as egg cups or ramekins, and bake in the oven for 15 minutes until just set.

Serve hot.

Tip: This recipe can be made with any type of edible mushroom or mushroom mixture. Shiitake mushrooms are particularly good.

FOR A FAMILY OF FOUR:
DOUBLE THE INGREDIENTS AND SERVE AS AN APPETIZER.

floating islands with peach melba swirl

These "floating islands" are made in the oven because it is so easy. However, you can also prepare them in almost-boiling water. Just add two or three scoops of the mixture at a time and "cook" them for a few minutes.

1 egg white
2 tablespoons sugar
pinch of salt
1 ripe peach
1/2–1 teaspoon honey
1/2 cup fresh or frozen raspberries

2–3 small portions

Preheat the oven to 210°F.

Beat the egg white with the sugar and a pinch of salt until very stiff. Cover a baking tray with baking parchment or foil, and place 6–9 spoonfuls of egg white on to the tray. Ensure there is plenty of space between them. Bake in the oven for about 1 1/2 hours.

Skin the peach and then whizz in a blender or food processor to a fine puree. If raspberry seeds are going to be a problem, you may want to pass the puree through a sieve. Sweeten with a little honey and pour into a small saucepan.

Wash the raspberries and dry them with paper towels. Place the raspberries in the blender or food processor (it doesn't have to be cleaned after the peaches). Whizz to a fine puree and sweeten with a little honey. Pour into another saucepan.

Heat both purees. Pour the peach puree into two or three small wide bowls. Add the raspberry puree and slide a knife through it to get the swirl effect. Place the egg-white "islands" on top.

Tip: To ensure that egg whites will properly stiffen when beaten, make certain the beaters used are grease-free by wiping them with paper towels sprinkled with vinegar.

FOR A FAMILY OF FOUR:
DOUBLE THE INGREDIENTS AND SERVE AS A DESSERT.

substituting ingredients

It isn't always necessary to follow recipes to the letter. If you don't have an ingredient, most of the time you can substitute it with something similar. For example, in this recipe, mango can be used instead of peach.

baked vanilla mousse

This recipe can also be made with chocolate but it will not be as light. To make chocolate mousse, do not use lemon juice. Melt 2 ounces chocolate with the cream and half a tablespoon of honey (instead of vanilla sugar) over a low heat.

1 egg
2 tablespoons custard powder
1/3 cup whipping cream or soy
   cream

2 tablespoons vanilla sugar
splash of lemon juice
pinch of salt

2 small portions

Preheat the oven to 325°F.

Separate the egg.

Mix the custard powder with 1 tablespoon of water.

Whisk the egg yolk with the custard powder, cream, vanilla sugar, and lemon juice until the sugar has dissolved.

Beat the egg white with a pinch of salt until stiff. Fold into the vanilla mixture.

Pour into two small greased oven dishes and bake in the oven for 20 minutes until just set.

Serve warm or cold.

Tip: Instead of vanilla sugar, you can use honey as a sweetener. In this case, add a drop of vanilla extract to the mixture.

FOR A FAMILY OF FOUR:
MULTIPLY THE RECIPE BY THREE AND SERVE AS A DESSERT.

warm cranberry and honey mousse

Sugarless cranberry juice is good for patients having abdominal radiotherapy, which affects the bladder and can cause radiation cystitis. However, cranberries can exaggerate the negative effects of warfarin (a blood thinner or anticoagulant) so don't use cranberry juice if you are taking warfarin.

scant $1/2$ cup cranberry juice
3 tablespoons honey
1 tablespoon cornstarch
2 egg whites
$1/3$ cup whipping cream or soy cream

2 small portions

Pour the cranberry juice into a pan. Add the honey, bring to a boil and reduce by half.

Mix the cornstarch with 1 tablespoon of water in a pan. Whisk in the egg whites, the cream, and the cranberry mixture.

Put the mixture in a double boiler or a bowl over simmering water and whisk until the mixture is thick and creamy, for about 5 minutes.

Divide between two glasses and serve immediately.

Tip: Cranberry juice can be bought ready-made or you can make it yourself by boiling cranberries with an equal amount of water. Strain and sweeten to taste. The cranberry juice can be replaced by other juices such as pomegranate, redcurrant, blueberry, or orange.

FOR A FAMILY OF FOUR:
MULTIPLY THE INGREDIENTS BY THREE
AND SERVE AS A DESSERT.

hot lemon mousse

In this recipe, the mousse is prepared in a double boiler and must be whisked for about 10 minutes. Make sure the pan with the lemon mixture is in a stable position so no water from the lower pan can get into it. The whisking can be done either by hand or with an electric mixer.

1 small lemon
1 tablespoon honey
1/2 tablespoon instant vanilla
    pudding
2 eggs
1/3 cup whipping or soya cream

2–3 small portions

Squeeze the lemon to obtain the juice and pour into the top pan of a double boiler and place directly on the burner. Add the honey, bring to a boil, and reduce by half. Place the pan over the bottom pan of a double boiler containing simmering water.

Mix the instant pudding with 1 tablespoon of water. Stir into the lemon mixture. Beat in the eggs and keep on beating until the mixture is thick and creamy, for 5–10 minutes.

Whip the cream and at the last moment, fold it into the lemon mousse.

Divide between two or three dishes and serve immediately.

Tip: Orange or lime juice can be used instead of lemon juice.

FOR A FAMILY OF FOUR:
MULTIPLY THE INGREDIENTS BY THREE AND SERVE AS A DESSERT.

special foods for different cancers

You should always consult your specialist and the oncology dietitian about what you should and shouldn't eat depending on your type of cancer.

chapter two
smooth

creamed asparagus and shrimp

Green asparagus may be used instead of white asparagus. The fresh dill can be left out or replaced with parsley, fennel, or chervil.

sprig of fresh dill
5 thin and small white asparagus,
    canned or freshly cooked
1/2 slice wholewheat bread
about 3/4 cup cooked shrimp
1 tablespoon mayonnaise
a few drops of fresh lemon juice
pinch of salt
pinch of pepper

2 small portions

Chop the dill very fine.

Peel the asparagus thinly, if using fresh, and snap off the woody part of the stems by bending the stalks until they break naturally. Cook the fresh asparagus in salted water for 10–15 minutes, until soft and then drain, reserving 2 tablespoons of the cooking water, and set aside to cool.

Whizz the bread in a blender or food processor into crumbs. Add the shrimp, asparagus, and 2 tablespoons of the cooking liquid if using fresh asparagus or 2 tablespoons of the liquid from the asparagus can if using canned. Whizz to a smooth cream. Mix in the mayonnaise, lemon juice, dill, a pinch of salt, and a pinch of pepper.

Fill two small glasses or bowls with the cream.

FOR A FAMILY OF FOUR:
MULTIPLY THE INGREDIENTS BY FOUR AND SERVE AS AN APPETIZER.

snacks

No matter which snacks you decide to serve, buy untreated products without preservatives where you can. Check the label for sugar content. Some of the best ready-to-eat smooth snacks include apple sauce, pudding, fruit yogurt, rhubarb compote, ripe kaki fruit (also called persimmon or Sharon fruit), ripe persimmons, and ripe melon.

avocado purée with orange

It is always best to buy avocados when they are really ripe; experience shows that they don't ripen easily later, and using them when they are still hard always leads to disappointment.

1 small ripe avocado
¼ cup orange juice
2 tablespoons sour
 or soy cream
pinch of salt
pinch of pepper

2–3 small portions

Cut the avocado in half. Remove the pit. Scoop out the pulp.

Whizz the avocado with the orange juice in a blender or food processor to a smooth cream. Fold in the sour cream or soy yogurt or mayonnaise. Add a pinch of salt and a pinch of pepper.

Fill two or three small glasses or dishes with the puree.

FOR A FAMILY OF FOUR:
DOUBLE THIS RECIPE AND SERVE AS AN APPETIZER.

puréed ratatouille

This recipe forms the basis for all sorts of vegetable dishes but it should always contain tomato. To accompany the tomato, choose vegetables with a firm texture such as carrot, broccoli, or celeriac (celery root). You can also add chopped herbs.

1 small tomato
1/8 red pepper
1/4 zucchini
1 small onion
1 garlic clove
1 small, sweet, pickled gherkin
2 tablespoons olive oil
salt and pepper
1/2 slice wholewheat bread
2 tablespoons sour cream
   (optional)

2 small portions

Wash the tomato, red pepper, and zucchini. Seed the red pepper. Peel the onion and the garlic. Chop the vegetables, onion, garlic, and gherkin into small pieces.

Heat the oil in a frying pan and fry the vegetables, onion, garlic, and gherkin for 3 minutes over a medium heat, stirring constantly. Add salt and pepper to taste. Add a scant cup of water, turn down the heat, and let the "ratatouille" simmer for 10 minutes.

Whizz the bread in a blender or food processor into crumbs. Add the ratatouille and whizz to a smooth cream. Let it cool. Adjust the seasoning.

Divide the ratatouille between two small glasses or dishes. Serve cold with, if you wish, a spoonful of sour cream.

FOR A FAMILY OF FOUR:
MULTIPLY THIS RECIPE BY FOUR AND SERVE AS AN APPETIZER.

shiitake mushroom cream

This cream can be enjoyed as it is, but it is also very nice with soft bread, on toast, or in a small crêpe. By simply adding some stock, you can easily turn it into a soup.

3 ounces mushrooms (button and some shiitake)
1/2 small onion
1/2 garlic clove
splash of olive oil
2 sprigs of fresh parsley

1/2 slice wholemeal bread
2 tablespoons crème fraîche or soy cream
salt and pepper

2 small portions

Wipe the mushrooms and chop them. Peel and chop the onion and garlic.

Heat a splash of olive oil in a big frying pan. Add the onion and mushrooms and fry for 5 minutes over a medium heat. Add the garlic and fry for another 3 minutes.

Chop the parsley fine.

Whizz the bread in a blender or food processor into crumbs. Add the mushrooms and parsley. Whizz to a smooth cream. Let it cool.

Add the crème fraîche to the mushroom cream and season to taste.

Fill two small dishes with the cream.

Tip: Instead of salt, a splash of soy sauce can be used to flavor this dish.

FOR A FAMILY OF FOUR:
MULTIPLY THE INGREDIENTS BY THREE AND SERVE AS AN APPETIZER.

minted tuna and peas

Should you want an even smoother cream, making it easier to swallow, strain this cream through a fine mesh strainer before adding mayonnaise.

3½ ounces fresh or frozen peas
sprig of fresh mint
⅓ cup freshly cooked
  or canned tuna

3 very small cocktail onions
1½ tablespoons mayonnaise

2 small portions

Cook the peas in boiling water for about 10 minutes until soft. Rinse with cold water and let cool.

Chop the mint leaves very fine.

Whizz the peas, tuna, cocktail onions, and mint in a blender or food processor to a smooth cream. Mix in the mayonnaise and a splash of the brine from the jar of onions.

Fill two small glasses or dishes with the cream.

Tip: As an alternative to tuna, you could use freshly cooked salmon or cooked shrimp in this recipe.

FOR A FAMILY OF FOUR:
MULTIPLY THE INGREDIENTS BY THREE AND SERVE AS AN APPETIZER.

panna cotta with honey and strawberries

This smooth and creamy pudding can be prepared up to two days in advance. However, its texture will stiffen slightly as time passes. The gelatin mixture should be cool but still fluid when adding it to the yogurt mixture. If it has already started to set, simply reheat it and so it will melt again.

1 1/2 teaspoons granulated gelatin
1/2 cup whipping cream or soy cream
2 tablespoons honey
2/3 cup plain or soy yogurt
6 strawberries

2–3 small portions

Prepare or soak the gelatin according to the instructions on the packet.

Bring half of the cream and all of the honey to a boil in a small saucepan. Stir and remove the pan from the heat. Stir in the gelatin and let it dissolve. Let cool, stirring every few minutes, until cool but not set.

Whip the remaining cream in the meantime until almost thick, and spoon in the yogurt quickly. Stir into the gelatin mixture. Mix well but do it quickly. Pour into two or three small bowls or glasses. Place in the fridge to set for at least 2 hours.

Clean and cut the strawberries in half, then sit them on the panna cottas.

Tip: Strawberries can be replaced with any other soft fruit you prefer, fresh or frozen.

FOR A FAMILY OF FOUR:
DOUBLE THIS RECIPE AND SERVE AS A DESSERT.

stop counting calories

During treatment, it does not make much sense to be counting calories. Because eating is already difficult enough, it is better to concentrate on using as wide a variety of healthy ingredients as possible.

soft apple and cinnamon compote

This compote can be made with apples or with a mixture of apples and blackberries, blueberries, or cranberries.

2 cooking apples
splash of lemon juice
$1/2$ tablespoon honey, or according to taste
pinch of cinnamon

2–3 small portions

Peel the apples, then halve, core and chop them.

Put the apples in a small saucepan with the lemon juice, honey, 3 tablespoons of water, and the cinnamon. Cook over medium heat for 5–8 minutes, until the compote is very soft, stirring now and then. Let cool.

Fill two small glasses or dishes with the compote and sprinkle with a little more cinnamon.

FOR A FAMILY OF FOUR:
MULTIPLY THE INGREDIENTS BY THREE AND SERVE AS A DESSERT.

banana and lemon mousse

A mousse like this is very quick and easy to prepare and you can use a wide variety of ripe fruit with a firm but soft texture. Hard fruits like apple and pear can also be used, but these have to be cooked first in a pan with a little water. You may use ready-made vanilla pudding or soy dessert instead of cream. If you do, don't add honey.

1 small lemon
1 ripe banana
$1/2$–1 tablespoon honey
scant $1/2$ cup whipping cream
   or soy cream

2–3 small portions

Squeeze the lemon. Peel the banana.

Whizz the banana with the honey and half the lemon juice in a blender or food processor to a fine puree. Add more lemon juice to taste.

Whip the cream and then fold into the banana puree.

Divide the mousse between two or three glasses and serve immediately.

FOR A FAMILY OF FOUR:
MULTIPLY THE INGREDIENTS BY THREE AND SERVE AS A DESSERT.

half-frozen fruit yogurt

You can make this sweet dish up to a day ahead but no earlier. It should then be taken out of the freezer to defrost for at least 30 minutes. If frozen fruits are used for the puree, the dish can also be served without freezing.

½ cup fresh or frozen mixed red fruit such as berries or cherries

2 tablespoons 100% fruit strawberry jam

⅓ cup tablespoons whipping cream or soy cream

½ cup plain or soy yogurt

2 small portions

Clean the fruit and whizz in a blender or food processor with the jam to a smooth puree.

Whip the cream until almost thick, and spoon the yogurt into it. Add the fruit puree and fold in gently so that the ingredients do not mix completely.

Divide the mixture between two small bowls or glasses and place in the freezer for 1–2 hours.

Tip: Instead of red fruit, try soft orange fruits such as apricots, peaches, or mangoes.

FOR A FAMILY OF FOUR:
MULTIPLY THE INGREDIENTS BY FOUR AND SERVE AS A DESSERT.

cauliflower cream with chicken patties

Cauliflower is rich in cancer-fighting nutrients, but it also releases a smell when it is cooked which can make chemo patients feel nauseous. One way to minimize the smell is to put unshelled walnuts or a slice of bread in the cooking water with the cauliflower. Alternatively, bake or steam it. Cooking cauliflower in an aluminum pot will intensify the unpleasant odor and turn it from creamy white to yellow; iron pots will turn it blue-green or brown.

5 small cauliflower florets
salt and pepper
3 sprigs of fresh parsley
1/2 slice wholewheat bread
1/4 cup finely chopped chicken
2 tablespoons light cream cheese

2 small portions

Cook the cauliflower in boiling water with a pinch of salt for about 8 minutes until soft. Drain well.

Chop the parsley very fine.

Whizz the bread with the parsley in a blender or food processor until it's crumbs. Mix the chopped chicken with 2 tablespoons of the breadcrumb mixture, a pinch of salt, a pinch of pepper, and a tablespoon of cream cheese. Divide into six portions and shape them into patties.

Place the patties in a single layer in the top of a steamer pan over boiling water. Cover the pan. Steam for 3–4 minutes until done.

Add the hot cauliflower in the meantime to the rest of the breadcrumbs and whizz to a smooth cream. Add the rest of the parsley and the cream cheese. Season with salt and pepper and reheat.

Put the patties and cauliflower, cream in two small bowls.

Tip: The chicken patties have a very soft and delicate texture, but if it is still too difficult to swallow the cooked patty, it may be whizzed in with the cauliflower. The chicken patties can also be cooked on a plate in the microwave; this will take a few minutes on full power.

FOR A FAMILY OF FOUR:
1 POUND, 10 OUNCES CAULIFLOWER, 4 SLICES WHOLEWHEAT BREAD, A SMALL BUNCH OF FRESH PARSLEY, 1 1/3 CUPS FINELY CHOPPED CHICKEN, 2/3 CUP LIGHT CREAM CHEESE. MIX THE CHICKEN WITH A QUARTER OF THE BREAD AND THE CREAM CHEESE. SERVE AS A MAIN COURSE.

scrambled egg with ham and chives

How you like your scrambled eggs is very personal. In this recipe it is better not to let them set too much in order to retain the creamy smoothness. Ham and chives can be entirely left out or substituted with smoked salmon (lox) and dill.

3 stems of fresh chives
1/2 slice wholewheat bread
1 thin slice ham
2 eggs
2 tablespoons butter
pinch of salt
pinch of pepper

2 small portions

Whizz the bread, the ham, and the chives in a blender or food processor until they're crumbs.

Beat the eggs a little and pour them into a small saucepan. Add the butter and the breadcrumbs. Cook over a low heat until the eggs have almost set, stirring regularly.

Add a pinch of salt and a pinch of pepper.

Divide between two small plates.

FOR A FAMILY OF FOUR:
MULTIPLY THE INGREDIENTS BY THREE AND SERVE IT FOR BREAKFAST.

"bubble and squeak" with bacon

This bubble and squeak is mashed very finely but it will still have some texture. For an even smoother result, pulse in a blender or food processor. Pulsing will ensure that the potatoes don't get sticky and leathery.

about 2¹/₂ cups cabbage
2 potatoes
salt and pepper
1 small onion
1 slice bacon

2 tablespoons olive oil
1¹/₂ tablespoons sour
 or soy cream

2 small portions

Wash the cabbage and cut it into small pieces. Peel the potatoes and cut them into 4 pieces. Put them in a small pan with the cabbage and a pinch of salt. Add just enough water to cover the vegetables. Cook for 15–20 minutes until the cabbage is very soft and the potatoes are done. Drain well.

Peel and finely chop the onion in the meantime. Cut the bacon into very small pieces.

Heat the oil in a frying pan and fry the onion and the bacon for 3 minutes over a low heat.

Add the onion and bacon to the strained potatoes and cabbage. Mash, or puree on the "pulse" setting in a blender or food processor until very fine. Stir in the cream and add salt and pepper to taste.

Divide between two small plates or bowls.

Tip: Adding a small apple (peeled, cored, and chopped) to this dish makes a nice change. Add the chopped apple to the pan 10 minutes before the potatoes are done.

FOR A FAMILY OF FOUR:
1 POUND, 10 OUNCES CABBAGE, 2¹/₄ POUNDS POTATOES, 2 BIG ONIONS, 6 SLICES BACON, ¹/₄ CUP OLIVE OIL, ¹/₃ CUP SOUR OR SOY CREAM. SERVE AS A MAIN COURSE.

potatoes and broccoli with trout

The smoky flavor of the trout gives this dish an intriguing taste. Other smoked ingredients are suitable, too, so you could also use other smoked fish, smoked ham, smoked bacon, or smoked sausage.

2 potatoes
salt and pepper
4 small broccoli florets
2½ ounces smoked trout fillet
3 stems of fresh chives
2 tablespoons sour or
   soy cream

2 small portions

Peel the potatoes and cut them into four pieces. Put them in a small pan with a pinch of salt. Add just enough water to cover them. Cook for 15–20 minutes or until the potatoes are done. Add the broccoli about 5 minutes before the potatoes are done. Drain well.

Chop the trout very finely. Remove any bones. Cut the chives very fine.

Mash the potatoes and broccoli very fine or pulse in a blender or food-processor. Add the trout and chives. Stir in the cream. Add salt and pepper to taste.

Tip: You may want to add the trout with the potatoes and broccoli when you puree or mash them together. This way it will get as finely chopped as the rest of the puree.

FOR A FAMILY OF FOUR:
2¼ POUNDS POTATOES, 1¼ POUNDS BROCCOLI, 4 SMOKED TROUT FILLETS, SMALL BUNCH OF FRESH CHIVES, ½ CUP SOUR OR SOY CREAM. SERVE AS A MAIN COURSE.

vegetable stew with cheese

The vegetables can be varied endlessly in this recipe, so you can make all sorts of combinations with your veggie favorites. If the dish is prepared in advance, add the cheddar after reheating and just before serving. It can also be made without cheese.

6 small carrots
6-inch piece of leek
2 potatoes
salt and pepper
1 garlic clove
1 tablespoon olive oil
2 tablespoons light cream cheese
2 tablespoons grated cheddar
    cheese

2 small portions

Peel and chop the carrots. Wash and finely chop the leek. Peel the potatoes and cut them into 4 pieces. Put the potatoes in a small pan with the carrots, the leek, and a pinch of salt. Add just enough water to cover the vegetables. Cook for 15–20 minutes until the carrots are very soft and the potatoes are done. Drain well.

Peel and chop the garlic. Heat the oil in a small frying pan and fry the garlic for 1 minute.

Add the garlic to the drained potatoes, leek, and carrots. Mash very fine, or pulse in a blender or food processor. Stir in the cream cheese and cheddar. Add salt and pepper to taste.

Divide between two small plates.

FOR A FAMILY OF FOUR:
18 OUNCES CARROTS, 4 LEEKS, $2^{1/4}$ POUNDS POTATOES, 3 GARLIC CLOVES, 2 TABLESPOONS OLIVE OIL, $^{1/2}$ CUP LIGHT CREAM CHEESE, $^{1/2}$ CUP GRATED CHEDDAR CHEESE. SERVE AS A MAIN COURSE.

experimenting

The recipes in this book are also intended to be a source of inspiration. Use your imagination, your preferred ingredients, and your kitchen experience to experiment.

warm pear cream

Try to avoid having too much sugar. If necessary, this cream can be sweetened to taste at the table with a little honey.

2 pear halves, freshly
   poached (see tip) or canned
   (containing as little added
   sugar as possible)
1/4 cup crème fraîche
   or soy cream
1/2 tablespoon instant vanilla
   pudding
1/2 teaspoon cinnamon

2 small portions

Whizz the pears in a blender or food-processor to a fine cream. Strain through a fine mesh strainer. Pour into a small saucepan and add the crème fraîche or cream. Bring to a boil.

Mix the instant pudding with a spoonful of liquid from the canned or poached pears. Stir into the pear mixture and let it thicken and cook over a low heat for a few minutes, stirring every now and then.

Pour into two cups, sprinkle with cinnamon, and serve right away.

Tip: To poach the pears, add 1 teaspoon of honey and a dash of lemon juice to every 1/2 cup of water. Peel and core the pears, and simmer in the poaching liquid for 10–20 minutes until soft.

FOR A FAMILY OF FOUR:
MULTIPLY THE INGREDIENTS BY FOUR AND SERVE AS A DESSERT.

warm or cold?
When asked what he or she would like to eat, a patient will often answer "something warm" or "something cold" so you will find both warm and cold recipes in each chapter.

honey custard

This recipe is very simple and just lovely as it is. However, you may choose to add other tasty ingredients such as ground hazelnuts or very finely chopped crystallized ginger in syrup instead of the honey. For a richer custard, you may substitute whipping or soy cream for a quarter of the milk.

1 cup lowfat milk or soy milk
2 tablespoons honey
1 tablespoon instant vanilla pudding

2 small portions

Pour 2 tablespoons of the milk into a cup and set aside. Bring the rest of the milk to a boil with half of the honey.

Mix the instant pudding in the cup with 2 tablespoons milk. Stir into the hot milk and let it thicken. Cook over a low heat for a few minutes, stirring every now and then.

Pour the warm custard into two small bowls and drizzle the rest of the honey on top.

FOR A FAMILY OF FOUR:
MULTIPLY THE INGREDIENTS BY THREE AND SERVE AS A DESSERT.

warm apricot smoothie

This type of smoothie can be made with all sorts of purees, using the fruit you have available. It is also possible to prepare this smoothie with dried apricots, fresh plums or prunes—just make sure the pits are out.

10 ripe fresh apricots
1 cup lowfat milk or soy milk
1/2 tablespoon honey
1/2 cup plain or soy yogurt

2–3 small portions

Wash the apricots and remove the pits.

Bring the milk to a boil with the apricots and honey. Let to simmer over a low heat for 5 minutes.

Put the apricots into a blender or food processor with a little of the milk and whizz to a smooth puree. Add the rest of the hot milk and whizz for another 2 minutes. Add the yogurt and whizz again.

Pour into two or three glasses or mugs.

FOR A FAMILY OF FOUR:
MULTIPLY THE INGREDIENTS BY FOUR AND SERVE AS A DESSERT.

steamed peach mousse

These mousses are served hot, but you can also let them cool down to serve lukewarm or cold. This will make the texture firmer. Try other fruit like apples or strawberries instead of peaches.

2 peach halves, freshly poached
(see tip page 66) or canned (containing
as little added sugar as possible)
2 tablespoons instant vanilla pudding
2 eggs
3 tablespoons whipping cream
or soy cream
2 tablespoons golden syrup

2–3 small portions

Whizz the peaches in a blender or food-processor to a fine puree.

Mix the instant pudding with 2 tablespoons of cold water. Whisk together the eggs, pudding, cream, and syrup until creamy, about 5 minutes. Fold in the peach puree.

Divide between two or three small ramekins. Cover with tinfoil. Place in the top of a steamer pan over boiling water. Cover the pan. Steam for about 10–15 minutes until just set. Remove and then take off the foil.

Place the ramekins on small plates and serve warm.

FOR A FAMILY OF FOUR:
DOUBLE THE INGREDIENTS AND SERVE AS A DESSERT.

eat what you can

What you can and may eat is a personal matter. Healthy food is always preferable, of course. But if it comes down to a choice between eating nothing or eating something like sugar, it's simple: have sugar and eat!

chapter three

soft with a bite

potato salad

To make this potato salad richer, you could add tiny pieces of ham or chopped cooked shrimp.

2 small potatoes
1 carrot
1 scallion
2 sprigs of fresh parsley
pinch of salt
1 egg
1 tablespoon mayonnaise
pinch of pepper

2 small portions

Peel the potatoes and cut them into small pieces. Peel the carrot and chop it fine. Wash the scallion and chop it finely. Chop the parsley.

Put the potatoes and the carrot in a pan. Add enough water to cover them and a pinch of salt. Bring the water to a boil and cook for 10–15 minutes or until the potatoes are ready. Add the chopped scallion and cook for 1 minute longer. Strain and set aside to cool.

Boil the egg for 8 minutes in boiling water. Hold it under cold water until it is cool enough to handle. Remove the shell and chop.

Mix the potatoes, carrot, and scallion with the egg, half of the parsley, and the mayonnaise. Adjust the seasoning.

Serve in two small bowls, sprinkled with the rest of the parsley.

Tip: Other fresh herbs like chives and celery leaf may be used instead of or in combination with the parsley.

FOR A FAMILY OF FOUR:
4 EGGS, 8 SMALL POTATOES,
6 CARROTS, 6 SCALLIONS,
A SMALL BUNCH OF PARSLEY,
1/2 CUP MAYONNAISE. SERVE
AS AN APPETIZER.

cream cheese and tomato sandwiches

It is healthier, if possible, to eat wholewheat bread. It should be soft but not too fresh, as that might make it more difficult to swallow. If the crusts are too hard, just cut them off.

1 ripe tomato
5 stems of fresh chives
2 slices wholewheat bread
1½ tablespoons light cream
   cheese

pinch of salt
pinch of pepper

2 small portions

Put the tomato in boiling water for 15 seconds. Rinse under a cold faucet and remove the skin. Cut the tomato in half and cut the flesh into strips.

Chop the chives very fine.

Cut the crusts off the bread if they are too hard.

Spread the slices of bread with the cream cheese.

Put the tomato strips on one slice of bread. Sprinkle with the chives, and season with a pinch each of salt and pepper.

Place the other slice of bread, cheese-side down, on the tomato. Cut the sandwich into fingers and put them on two small plates.

Tip: The tomato may be replaced by avocado or banana. If banana is used, leave out the chives, salt, and pepper.

FOR A FAMILY OF FOUR:
MULTIPLY THE INGREDIENTS BY FOUR.

melon and feta salad

To make this recipe work, choose a ripe, sweet melon with a nice aromatic smell. If you cannot find a ripe melon, it's better to use a different fruit, such as a ripe mango or even strawberries. The feta can be left out, and fried bacon bits may be added.

1 scallion
sprig of fresh parsley
about 1-ounce feta cheese cubes
1 tablespoon lemon juice
2 tablespoons flaxseed or olive oil
pinch of salt
pinch of pepper
1/2 very small cantaloupe melon

2–3 small portions

Wash and chop the scallion fine. Chop the parsley fine. Crumble the feta cheese.

Mix the scallion with the parsley, lemon juice, oil, and a pinch each of salt and pepper.

Cut the melon into three wedges and scoop out the seeds. Scoop the flesh out of the melon, reserving the skins, and cut the flesh into pieces and place in a bowl.

Mix the feta and scallion dressing thoroughly with the melon. Place each melon skin wedge on a small plate and spoon 2–3 good tablespoons of melon salad over it.

Tip: This melon salad can be kept in the fridge for at least a day, so there is no need to finish it all in one go.

FOR A FAMILY OF FOUR:
DOUBLE THE INGREDIENTS AND SERVE AS AN APPETIZER.

snacks

Recommended "fast" soft snacks with a bite are shop-bought profiteroles with custard or cream, ripe cherry tomatoes, grapes or cherries and ripe soft fruits. You could also put a lot of different soft fruits together in a delicious fresh fruit salad.

mushroom and tomato pasta salad

The fettucine in this recipe can be replaced with any other dried or pre-cooked pasta—but just make sure you cook your pasta slightly longer than normal to obtain the recommended soft texture.

2 cherry tomatoes
6 small mushrooms
2 small broccoli florets
2 green beans
2 sun-dried tomatoes in olive oil
2 ounces fettucine

salt and pepper
2 teaspoons vinegar
pinch of sugar

2–3 small portions

Wash the vegetables. Cut the cherry tomatoes, mushrooms, broccoli, beans, and sun-dried tomatoes into small pieces.

Cook the pasta in boiling water with a pinch of salt for 2 minutes longer than the suggested time on the package. Add the pieces of broccoli and beans 5 minutes before the end of the cooking time. Strain.

Heat a small frying pan and add 2 tablespoons of oil from the sun-dried tomatoes. Add the mushrooms and fry for 2 minutes over a low heat. Add the pieces of cherry tomato and sun-dried tomato. Stir in the vinegar, sugar, and salt and pepper to taste. Turn off the heat.

Mix all the ingredients together and let the pasta salad cool. Serve in two or three small bowls.

Tip: This pasta salad can be kept in the fridge for about a day, so there is no need to finish it all in one go.

FOR A FAMILY OF FOUR:
6 CHERRY TOMATOES, 9 OUNCES MUSHROOMS, 1 HEAD BROCCOLI,
2/3 CUP GREEN BEANS, 6 SUN-DRIED TOMATOES, 11 OUNCES FETTUCINE,
1/3 CUP OIL FROM THE SUN-DRIED TOMATOES, 2 TABLESPOONS VINEGAR,
SUGAR, SALT, AND PEPPER TO TASTE.

eggplant and chicken spread sandwich

This sandwich can also be made with a zucchini and it's equally nice with smoked ham or smoked salmon.

¹/₄ eggplant
¹/₂ tablespoon olive oil
sprig of fresh parsley
about 1-ounce piece
    of smoked chicken
1 tablespoon light cream
    cheese or fresh cheese

pinch of pepper
1 cherry tomato
4 small lettuce leaves

2 small portions

Wash the eggplant and slice into four rounds. Sprinkle with olive oil and fry in a frying pan until brown on both sides. Set aside to cool.

Chop the parsley.

Whizz the chicken with the cream cheese in a blender or food processor until smooth. Add a pinch of pepper and   the parsley.

Cut the cherry tomato into six tiny wedges.

Spoon a teaspoon of chicken spread onto a slice of eggplant. Wash the lettuce leaves and then put two of them, half the remaining chicken spread, and half the tomato wedges on top. Cover with a second eggplant slice and repeat with the remaining ingredients.

Serve on two small plates.

Tip: The eggplant may be peeled and the tomato skinned, if necessary.

FOR A FAMILY OF FOUR:
DOUBLE THE INGREDIENTS AND SERVE AS AN APPETIZER.

quick frozen raspberry and custard dessert

You can buy the vanilla pudding for this recipe ready-made or you can make it up from a box of instant vanilla pudding, but it should be cold before using.

5 ounces frozen raspberries
2/3 cup ready-made vanilla pudding
1–2 tablespoons raspberry syrup

2 small portions

Whizz the raspberries in a blender or food processor. Make sure the mixture is as fine as possible but still frozen.

Mix in the pudding and the syrup to taste.

Spoon into two glasses or bowls and serve immediately.

Tip: You could use blackberries instead of raspberries.

FOR A FAMILY OF FOUR:
MULTIPLY THE INGREDIENTS BY THREE AND SERVE AS A DESSERT.

choose untreated

Weedkillers and insecticides have adverse effects on the immune system. It's therefore always best to choose untreated (ecological) ingredients. Always wash fruit and vegetables well whether organic or not, to kill *E. coli* bacteria.

berry jello

To make sure you get as many vitamins as possible, the whole fruit is used for this jello. As a result, the jello is not as clear as the store-bought kind.

7 ounces strawberries
5 ounces blueberries
2 teaspoons granulated gelatin
   or 3 gelatine leaves
1 tablespoon honey

2–3 small portions

Wash the fruit. Set aside a strawberry and two blueberries.

Whizz the remaining strawberries and blueberries in a blender or food processor. Make sure the mixture is as fine as possible so strain it through a fine mesh strainer.

Prepare or soak the gelatin according to the instructions on the package.

Put a quarter of the fruit puree into a small saucepan with the honey. Bring to a boil, then remove the pan from the heat. Stir in the gelatin and let it dissolve, then stir in the rest of the fruit puree. Pour into two or three glasses.

Leave it in the fridge to set for at least 2 hours.

Cut the remaining strawberry into four wedges. Garnish the jello with strawberry wedges and blueberries.

Tip: This type of jello can also be made with a single ripe fruit or other combination of fruit. Try mangoes, melons, peaches, nectarines, apricots, plums, grapes, cherries, redcurrants, and other berries.

FOR A FAMILY OF FOUR:
MULTIPLY THE INGREDIENTS BY FOUR AND SERVE AS A DESSERT.

creamy rice pudding with cranberries

As with most recipes, this rice pudding is sweetened with honey because that is considered healthier than white sugar.

scant cup lowfat or soy milk
2 tablespoons instant short-grain rice
2 tablespoons half-dried cranberries

1–1$\frac{1}{2}$ tablespoons honey
$\frac{1}{2}$ cup whipping cream or soy cream

2–3 small portions

Bring the milk to a boil in a small saucepan with the rice, cranberries, and honey to taste. Turn down the heat as low as possible and let it simmer until the rice is soft, stirring occasionally. The cooking time varies with the brand of rice so check the package instructions.

Set aside to cool, stirring occasionally.

Whip the cream until almost stiff and fold into the cold rice pudding.

Divide between two or three small bowls or glasses.

Tip: The cranberries can be replaced by other dried fruits like apples, prunes, figs, apricots, or raisins.

FOR A FAMILY OF FOUR:
MULTIPLY THE INGREDIENTS BY THREE AND SERVE AS A DESSERT.

honeyed fruit salad

This fruit salad is served with a lemon and honey dressing. For some people, it may be a bit too acidic. If that's the case, use a bottled fruit syrup instead.

1/2 small lemon
1/2 tablespoon honey
1 banana
1 peach or nectarine, fresh
   or canned (containing as little
   added sugar as possible)
1 kiwi fruit

2–3 small portions

Squeeze the lemon juice into a big bowl. Add the honey and stir until it has dissolved.

Peel the banana. Remove the skin from the peach and the kiwi fruit. Cut the peach in half and remove the pit.

Cut the fruit into small pieces and mix them with the honey mixture. Let rest for at least 10 minutes.

Divide between two or three glasses or bowls.

Tip: Most fruits can easily be mixed with others. It is best to use ripe soft fruits when they are in season.

FOR A FAMILY OF FOUR:
MULTIPLY THE INGREDIENTS BY THREE AND SERVE AS A DESSERT.

mint and ginger

Some natural ingredients have medicinal properties that ease nausea and stomach ache. In mild cases of nausea, try some mint tea or fresh ginger (used in dishes or in ginger tea)—they will offer some relief.

chicken ragoût

Ragoûts are nice and smooth and often go down well. The chicken in this recipe can be replaced with a good, fresh ham without preservatives from your local butcher, or with cooked fish or shrimp. If you use fish or shrimp, you may want to use fish stock.

scant $2/3$ cup instant whole-grain rice
4 green beans
$1/8$ red pepper
2 scallions
pinch of salt
2 ounces cooked or smoked chicken
1 tablespoon olive oil
2 teaspoons flour
scant cup chicken stock made
    with a stock cube or homemade
2 tablespoons crème fraîche
    or soy cream
pinch of pepper

2 small portions

Cook the rice in boiling water following the instructions on the package. Drain.

Wash the beans and slice them very thinly. Wash and deseed the red pepper. Wash the scallions and chop into very small pieces.

Cook the beans and red pepper for 8 minutes in boiling water with a pinch of salt. Add the scallions after 5 minutes and cook together for another 3 minutes. Drain.

Cut the chicken into small pieces.

Heat the olive oil in a saucepan. Remove from the heat and stir in the flour. Heat for 3 minutes, stirring occasionally. Remove from the heat again and stir in half of the stock. Bring to a boil, stirring continuously, adding more stock when the sauce gets thicker. When all the stock is used, add the vegetables and the chicken.

Stir in the crème fraîche or soy cream and let it cook over a low heat for a few minutes. Season.

Serve the rice with the ragoût on two small plates.

Tip: Rice is not easy to eat for everyone who is ill. It can be replaced by pasta or potatoes.

FOR A FAMILY OF FOUR:
$1^1/2$ CUPS INSTANT WHOLE-GRAIN RICE, 14 OUNCES GREEN BEANS, 2 RED PEPPERS, 8 SCALLIONS, 11 OUNCES COOKED OR SMOKED CHICKEN, $1/3$ CUP OLIVE OIL, 3 TABLESPOONS FLOUR, 4 CUPS CHICKEN STOCK, $1/2$ CUP CRÈME FRAÎCHE, SALT AND PEPPER TO TASTE.

onion sizes

The ingredients lists in this book frequently include "a small onion." This refers to an onion about $1^1/2$ inches wide. Scallions should weigh about $2/3$ ounce.

macaroni with leek, ham, and cheese

This macaroni can be finished in the oven or under the broiler, with some extra cheese "au gratin" on top. Don't let it get too crispy, though, since that might make it hard to swallow.

$1/3$–$1/2$ cup macaroni
about 4-inch piece of leek
1 small tomato
about a 1-ounce slice fresh ham without
    preservatives, from the butcher
2 sprigs of fresh parsley
2 tablespoons olive oil
2 tablespoons light cream cheese
2 tablespoons grated cheddar cheese
pinch of salt
pinch of pepper

2 small portions

Cook the macaroni in boiling water following the package instructions. Drain.

Wash the leek and cut into very thin slices. Wash the tomato and cut into small pieces. Cut the ham into fine strips. Chop the parsley.

Heat the olive oil in a saucepan and fry the leek for 3 minutes over a medium heat. Add the tomato and fry for another minute.

Add the cream cheese and let it melt. Stir in the grated cheddar and heat until melted. Add the macaroni, ham, half the parsley, and season to taste with a pinch each of salt and pepper. Heat for 1 minute longer.

Serve on two small plates and sprinkle with the rest of the parsley.

Tip: Leeks taste not only great, but also provide some extra color to the dish, which helps in the appreciation of the food. If there are no leeks available, onions can be used instead.

FOR A FAMILY OF FOUR:
$2^2/3$ CUPS MACARONI, 3 LEEKS, 6 TOMATOES, 7 OUNCES HAM, A SMALL BUNCH OF PARSLEY, $1/4$ CUP OLIVE OIL, SCANT CUP CREAM CHEESE, $1/2$ CUP GRATED CHEDDAR CHEESE, SALT AND PEPPER TO TASTE.

oriental rice
with fruit and nuts

The flavor of this aromatic, sweet and savoury rice may be enriched by adding a thread of saffron (soaked in a teaspoon of hot water). A cardamom seed can also be used. Both ingredients should be put in at the same time as the dried fruits.

1 orange
1 tablespoon honey
2 dried apricots
2 prunes
2 pieces dried apple
about 4-inch piece of leek

1/4 cup mixed nuts
  (but not peanuts)
2/3 cup instant whole-grain rice
1 tablespoon olive oil
1/2 vegetable bouillon cube
1 teaspoon cinnamon

2 small portions

Wash the orange and grate the zest coarsely into a small saucepan. Cut it in half and squeeze all of the orange juice into the pan. Add the honey and cook for 2 minutes over a medium heat. Set aside to cool.

Chop the dried fruits, leek, and nuts fine. Wash the rice.

Heat the olive oil in a small saucepan. Fry the leek for 3 minutes over a low heat. Stir in the rice, fruits, nuts, 1 1/4 cups water, and the bouillon cube.

Cook the rice over a very low heat until dry and soft (according to the package instructions). If the rice is dry but not yet soft, add a little more hot water and cook until done.

Mix in the cinnamon. Serve the rice on two small plates and add the orange and honey syrup to taste.

Tip: Since it spoils easily, make just enough cooked rice and eat it when fresh.

FOR A FAMILY OF FOUR:
2 ORANGES, 2 TABLESPOONS HONEY, 5 OUNCES DRIED FRUITS, 2 LEEKS, 3/4 CUP NUTS, 1 3/4 CUPS INSTANT WHOLE-GRAIN RICE, 3 TABLESPOONS OLIVE OIL, 1 1/2 BOUILLON CUBES, 6 CUPS WATER, 4 TEASPOONS CINNAMON.

stir-fried chicken noodles

For this dish you can choose between egg noodles, rice noodles, and special stir-fry noodles. You can easily change the vegetables and chicken to whatever combination you prefer. To make it a vegetarian meal, replace the chicken with pieces of omelet or tofu.

about 1³/₄ ounces noodles
1 small lemon
4 scallions
¹/₄ red pepper
6 shiitake mushrooms
1³/₄-ounce piece chicken breast

1 tablespoon olive oil
1 tablespoon sweet thick soy
  sauce
salt and pepper

2–3 small portions

Cook the noodles in boiling water for 1 minute longer than the suggested time on the package. Strain and set aside to cool.

Wash the lemon and grate the zest coarsely (you will need 2 small teaspoons of zest). Cut the lemon in half.

Wash the scallions and red pepper and wipe the mushrooms. Seed the red pepper and chop all the vegetables into small pieces.

Cut the chicken into small strips.

Heat the oil in a wok. Add the chicken and stir-fry over a low heat for 3 minutes. Add the vegetables and stir-fry for another 5 minutes. Mix in the noodles and the lemon zest and stir-fry a little bit longer until the noodles are hot. Add the soy sauce and squeeze a little bit of lemon juice over the dish. Season.

Serve the noodles in two or three small bowls. A wedge of lemon may be added.

Tip: Cooked noodles can be kept in the fridge for about a day. However, they are at their best when freshly cooked.

FOR A FAMILY OF FOUR:
11 OUNCES NOODLES, ZEST AND JUICE OF 1 LEMON, 8 SCALLIONS, 2 RED PEPPERS, 9 OUNCES SHIITAKE MUSHROOMS, 7 OUNCES CHICKEN BREAST, 2 TABLESPOONS OLIVE OIL, SWEET, THICK SOY SAUCE TO TASTE.

grilled pepper and cheese crêpes

These crêpes can also be served with a choice of sweet toppings but to do so, you may want to add some vanilla sugar to the batter.

1/4 cup wholewheat flour
pinch of salt
scant 1/2 cup lowfat milk
   or soy milk
3 tablespoons beaten egg
1 grilled pepper from a jar
sprig of fresh parsley

splash of olive oil
2 tablespoons tomato ketchup
   or tomato sauce
3 tablespoons grated cheddar
   cheese

2 small portions

Mix the flour, a pinch of salt, and the milk and egg together and whisk until the batter is smooth.

Cut the pepper into strips. Chop the parsley.

Heat a splash of olive oil in a big frying pan. Place two spoonfuls of batter in the pan, allowing room to spread, and fry the crêpes for a few minutes until dry on top and light brown on the other side. Flip them over and spread with the tomato ketchup or sauce.

Place the pepper strips on top and sprinkle with the grated cheese. Fry for another minute over a low heat until the cheese has melted.

Place the crêpes on two small plates and sprinkle with the parsley.

Tip: If you cannot or do not want to eat cheddar cheese, you don't have to use it. You can use light cream cheese instead.

FOR A FAMILY OF FOUR:
MULTIPLY THE INGREDIENTS BY FOUR AND SERVE FOR LUNCH.

oatmeal porridge with almonds and honey

The right thickness of oatmeal porridge is a matter of personal preference. In order to make it thicker or thinner, you simply add more or less rolled oats. Should it still be too thick, just add some more milk and heat the oatmeal a while longer.

1 cup lowfat milk or soy milk
1/3 cup rolled oats
pinch of salt
2 tablespoons ground almonds
1–2 tablespoons honey
2 tablespoons whipping
    or soy cream

2 small portions

Bring the milk, oats, a pinch of salt, and the almonds slowly to a boil over a medium heat. Keep stirring until the oatmeal starts to get thick and creamy, then turn down the heat and let it cook for a few minutes longer.

Divide the oatmeal between two bowls and top with the honey and cream. Stir a bit before serving.

Tip: As a welcome variation, the oatmeal can be sweetened with all sorts of ingredients such as 100% fruit jam or fresh sweet fruit.

FOR A FAMILY OF FOUR:
MULTIPLY THE INGREDIENTS BY FOUR.

textures to suit the situation

Patients may prefer different textures during the various stages of chemotherapy, depending on the effects of their treatment at any particular time. This might mean that sometimes they can enjoy any of the textures here, while at other times, perhaps only one certain texture will appeal.

fried banana and maple cream

This is a recipe for one of those days when you don't feel like being good and you want to indulge yourself. Use pineapple or apple as an alternative to the banana if you wish. Even after cooking, the texture of pineapple is not as soft as that of banana, so only choose this variation if it is possible for the patient to swallow firm textures.

$1/2$ cup whipping cream
$1/4$ cup maple syrup
1 banana
1 tablespoon butter

2 small portions

Whip the cream with 1 tablespoon of maple syrup until almost stiff.

Peel the banana and cut into thick slices.

Melt the butter in a frying pan and cook the slices of banana for 1–2 minutes on each side until brown. Add the rest of the maple syrup and heat for a $1/2$ minute more.

Place the banana slices in two small bowls and spoon some maple cream and the hot maple syrup from the pan over it.

Tip: In this book, olive oil is usually recommended for frying instead of butter. However, in this recipe butter is preferred.

FOR A FAMILY OF FOUR:
MULTIPLY THE INGREDIENTS BY FOUR AND SERVE AS A DESSERT.

jam crêpes with vanilla sugar

For this recipe it is best to use jam made with 100% fruit. If not available, any other jam can be used provided it is not overly sweet.

2 tablespoons wholewheat flour
$^1/_2$ tablespoon vanilla sugar
pinch of salt
$^1/_3$ cup lowfat or soy milk
1 tablespoon whisked egg
splash of mild olive oil
2 tablespoons 100% fruit jam
1 teaspoon confectioners' sugar

2 small portions

Mix the flour, vanilla sugar, salt, milk, and egg together and stir until the batter is smooth.

Heat a splash of olive oil in a small frying pan. Pour half of the batter into the pan and fry the crêpe for a few minutes until dry on top and light brown on the other side.

Flip over and fry for another minute or so until light brown. Slide on to a plate and repeat with the remaining batter to make a second crêpe.

Place the crêpes on two small plates. Spread with the jam, roll up, and dust with the confectioners' sugar.

Tip: These crêpes may be served with a scoop of ice cream or some fresh fruit.

FOR A FAMILY OF FOUR:
MULTIPLY THE INGREDIENTS BY SIX AND SERVE AS A DESSERT.

stewed fruit with ice cream

Since dried fruits keep so well, they are ideal to have on hand so that you can quickly prepare a dish when it's needed. However, you can also use fresh fruit, if you have it, for this recipe—just make sure that you wash them before you use them.

2 prunes
2 ready-to-eat dried apricots
1 tablespoon dried cranberries
   or raisins
1/2 lemon
1/2–1 tablespoon honey
1 teaspoon arrowroot
2 scoops ice cream

2 small portions

Cut the prunes, apricots, and cranberries into pieces.

Squeeze the juice from the lemon into a saucepan. Add scant 1/2 cup water and honey to taste, and bring to a boil. Stir until the honey is dissolved. Add the prunes, apricots, and cranberries or raisins, and cook for 5 minutes over a low heat.

Mix the arrowroot with 1/2 a tablespoon of cold water and stir it into the fruit mixture. Cook for 2 minutes.

Scoop the ice cream onto two small dishes and spoon the warm fruit stew next to it.

FOR A FAMILY OF FOUR:
MULTIPLY THE INGREDIENTS BY FOUR AND SERVE AS A DESSERT.

a little at a time
Big portions of food can easily put patients off, so it's better to serve several small portions of food at different times throughout the day.

chapter four

liquid

chilled carrot and citrus soup

This smooth and creamy soup can be made thinner or thicker to your liking.
Just add more or less stock. Like most cold soups, it can also be served warm.

1/2 slice wholewheat bread
4 carrots
1 small onion
1 small lemon
1 small orange
2 stems of fresh chives
  (optional)
3 tablespoons olive oil

2/3 cup lowfat chicken
  stock from a cube
  or homemade
1/3 cup whipping cream
  or soy cream
salt and pepper

2 small portions

Cut off the crusts and cut the bread in cubes. Peel and
chop the carrots and onion. Wash and zest the lemon.
Squeeze the juice out of half of the lemon and all of the
orange. Wash and chop the chives fine.

Heat the olive oil in a saucepan. Add the carrots, the onion,
and the lemon zest. Fry for 3 minutes over a medium heat.
Add the bread cubes, 1/2 tablespoon of lemon juice, the
lemon and orange juice, and the stock. Cook for 10–15
minutes until the carrots are very soft. Add the cream and
cook for a further minute.

Whizz in a blender or food-processor. Make sure the soup
is completely smooth. Add salt and pepper to taste and let
cool. Keep the soup in the fridge until needed.

Pour into two glasses or bowls and sprinkle with chives,
if using, and some extra lemon zest.

Tip: For this recipe it is also very nice to use pumpkin
or zucchini instead of carrots.

FOR A FAMILY OF FOUR:
MULTIPLY THE INGREDIENTS BY THREE AND SERVE AS AN APPETIZER.

cucumber and apple smoothie

This smoothie can be made with all sorts of fruit juice. The yogurt can also be omitted and replaced by a similar amount of fruit juice.

1/2 cucumber
1/4 slice wholewheat bread
2 fresh mint leaves
2/3 cup live or soy yogurt
scant 1/2 cup apple juice

pinch of salt
pinch of pepper

2 small portions

Peel and chop the cucumber. Cut off the crusts and cut the bread into pieces.

Whizz all the ingredients in a blender or food-processor. Make sure the mixture is as smooth as possible.

Pour into two glasses and serve immediately or leave it in the fridge until needed.

Tip: 1/2 tablespoon of honey can be added to sweeten this smoothie. However, it is better to avoid the sugar, if you can resist it.

FOR A FAMILY OF FOUR:
MULTIPLY THE INGREDIENTS BY THREE.

savory raspberry gazpacho

Traditionally, this cold soup is prepared with tomatoes (very nice and highly recommended) but this variation with raspberries is even more appreciated by both sick people and their family members. Variations on this gazpacho can also be made with strawberries, blackberries, or blueberries.

1/2 cucumber
1/2 shallot or small onion
1 small garlic clove
1/4 slice wholewheat bread
1/3 cup olive oil
1–2 teaspoons raspberry
   or balsamic vinegar
5 ounces frozen or fresh
   raspberries
salt and pepper
1/2–1 tablespoon raspberry syrup

2 small portions

Peel the cucumber, the shallot or onion, and the garlic. Cut off the crusts and cut the bread into cubes.

Whizz all the ingredients except for 2 raspberries and the seasonings in a blender or food-processor with 3 tablespoons of cold water. Make sure the mixture is as smooth as possible. Season with salt and pepper and add raspberry syrup to taste.

Pour into two glasses or bowls, put a raspberry in the middle, and serve immediately or leave in the fridge until needed.

Tip: Adding a dash of Tabasco is very nice but could be too strong. Therefore it's best to let those who like spicy food add Tabasco themselves, to taste.

FOR A FAMILY OF FOUR:
DOUBLE THE INGREDIENTS AND SERVE AS AN APPETIZER.

snacks
Recommended ready-to-eat liquid snacks are tomato or mixed vegetable juice (especially fresh carrot juice which is excellent), fruit juices, breakfast drinks, and smoothies. Look out for juices without added sugar; you can always spice them up at home if necessary.

chilled tomato and red pepper soup

A quick and easy cold soup that doesn't need any cooking. It can also be served hot.

¹/₂ slice wholewheat bread
2 grilled red peppers from a jar
sprig of fresh parsley or a few
   fresh basil leaves
1 cup tomato juice
2 tablespoons olive oil
salt and pepper

2 small portions

Cut off the crusts and cut the bread into cubes.

Whizz all the ingredients in a blender or food-processor. Make sure the mixture is as smooth as possible.

Pour into two glasses or bowls. Serve immediately or leave in the fridge until needed.

Tip: Red peppers in a jar often taste very nice and a little of the liquid can be added to the soup to enhance the flavor. If you prefer to broil the peppers yourself, you'll find instructions on page 38.

FOR A FAMILY OF FOUR:
MULTIPLY THIS RECIPE BY THREE AND SERVE AS AN APPETIZER.

spinach and walnut smoothie

Smoothies can be made with vegetables or fruit or a mixture of both—the possibilities are endless. And since they are nutritious as well as quick and easy to prepare, they're ideal as an "instant" liquid meal. They are usually made with milk, buttermilk, or yogurt, but if dairy products don't go down well, try avocado purée, tomato juice or carrot juice.

2 ounces fresh spinach
2 tablespoons shelled walnuts
1 cup buttermilk

1/2–1 tablespoon honey
salt and pepper

2–3 small portions

Wash and dry the spinach thoroughly.

Whizz the spinach, walnuts, buttermilk, and honey in a blender or food-processor. Make sure the mixture is as smooth as possible. Season.

Pour into two or three glasses and serve immediately or leave in the fridge until needed.

Tip: In this recipe, fresh spinach can be replaced with frozen spinach. Let it defrost first or, to make a really cold smoothie, whizz it 10 minutes after you've taken it out of the freezer.

FOR A FAMILY OF FOUR:
MULTIPLY THE INGREDIENTS BY THREE
AND SERVE AS A DRINK.

almond and peach smoothie

Soft fruits such as peaches are ideal for smoothies like this one. However, the fruits must be ripe. The same goes for apricots, plums, melon, mango, bananas, and all sorts of berries.

2 ripe peaches
1/3 cup peach syrup
1/4 cup ground almonds
scant cup lowfat or soy milk

2 small portions

Peel and pit the peaches.

Whizz all the ingredients in a blender or food-processor. Make sure the mixture is as smooth as possible.

Pour into two glasses and serve immediately or place in the fridge until needed.

Tip: This smoothie can also be made with canned peaches, using the syrup from the can. If milk is a problem, replace it with fruit juice.

FOR A FAMILY OF FOUR:
MULTIPLY THE INGREDIENTS BY THREE AND SERVE AS A DRINK.

the challenge

Cooking for somebody with cancer can be very rewarding but also very disappointing. All you want is the patient to appreciate the food, eat well, and keep strong. However, it could easily be that the patient can't eat any of the dishes you have so carefully prepared. Unfortunately, this is just part of the reality. Try to accept it with as light a spirit as possible because it is frustrating not only for the cook but also for the patient.

ice cold strawberry and cranberry juice

The strawberries used in this recipe are frozen. Take them out of the freezer 10 minutes before using so they will be easier to puree.

9 ounces frozen strawberries,
   slightly thawed
1/3 cup sugar-free cranberry juice

2 small portions

Whizz the strawberries in a blender or food-processor to   a very fine purée. Add the cranberry juice. Whizz for a minute longer.

Pour into two glasses and serve immediately.

Tip: To sweeten this cold juice, some honey may be added.

FOR A FAMILY OF FOUR:
MULTIPLY THE INGREDIENTS BY THREE AND SERVE AS A DRINK.

chilled mixed fruit soup

You could replace the melon, tangerine, and kiwi fruit combination with all sorts of other fruity combinations, such as melon, plums, and raspberries; banana, kiwi, and mango; nectarine, redcurrants, and passion fruit; or pear, blackberries, and orange.

1 small wedge of ripe melon
2 tangerines
1 ripe kiwi fruit
1 tablespoon honey

1–2 small portions

Peel the fruit.

Whizz all the ingredients in a blender or food-processor. Make sure the mixture is as smooth as possible.

Strain the juice.

Pour into one or two small bowls and serve immediately or leave in the fridge until needed.

Tip: This fruit soup can be diluted by adding some fruit juice, to taste.

FOR A FAMILY OF FOUR:
MULTIPLY THE INGREDIENTS BY FOUR AND SERVE AS A DESSERT.

make it special

Try to treat eating as a social event, especially when the chemotherapy is having side effects and patients are feeling less and less like eating. This will hopefully encourage them to eat more. Always prepare at least two portions. The extra portion can be kept in the fridge for at least another day, to be eaten at another time.

banana and ginger milkshake

Milkshakes are delicious, creamy, and cold, and often go down easily. However, since they contain milk, ice cream, or dairy products, they may cause problems. If so, use fruit juice and sherbet instead of milk and ice cream.

1 banana
a marble-sized piece fresh ginger
1/4 cup ginger syrup
1 tablespoon fresh lime juice
3 scoops of vanilla ice cream
scant 1/2 cup lowfat milk or soy milk

2 small portions

Peel the banana and ginger. Grate the ginger fine.

Whizz the banana with the grated ginger, the ginger syrup, and the lime juice to a very smooth puree in a blender or food processor.

Add the ice cream and milk and whizz for a few more minutes.

Pour into two glasses and serve immediately or leave in the fridge until needed.

Tip: For a comparable milkshake, all types of soft fruits may be used. Lime juice can be replaced by lemon or orange juice, and ginger syrup by any 100% fruit jam. Fresh ginger can be left out, so this is a very flexible recipe.

FOR A FAMILY OF FOUR:
MULTIPLY THE INGREDIENTS BY THREE.

be flexible
Since appetite may come and go within minutes, try not to be disappointed or too pushy if the food you have prepared is rejected.

fennel soup with cream

This soup is best when very smooth and creamy. If it isn't as smooth as you expected, it can be strained before serving. The bread used in creamy soups can be left out if the patient cannot tolerate it.

1/2 slice wholewheat bread
1 bulb fennel
1 small onion
3 tablespoons olive oil
1 cup chicken stock from a stock cube
    or homemade
1/3 cup whipping cream or soy cream
salt and pepper

2 small portions

Remove the crusts and cut the bread into cubes. Wash and chop the fennel, then set the fronds aside. Peel and chop the onion.

Heat the olive oil in a saucepan. Add the fennel and the onion and fry for 3 minutes over a medium heat. Add the bread and the stock. Cook until the fennel is very soft, 15–20 minutes. Add the cream and cook for another minute.

Whizz to a smooth soup in a blender or food-processor. Add salt and pepper to taste.

Ladle into two bowls and sprinkle with the fennel fronds.

Tip: This recipe is also delicious with celery or cucumber instead of fennel.

FOR A FAMILY OF FOUR:
DOUBLE THE INGREDIENTS AND SERVE AS AN APPETIZER.

wholewheat wheat

Wholewheat bread is used a lot in the recipes. Among other things, it helps the digestive system. However, it will not necessarily be good for everybody. With people suffering from intestine or stomach problems, it might trigger cramps, since wholewheat is more difficult to digest. If so, use white bread instead. If that causes digestive problems too, you can leave the bread out of most recipes.

chicken and tomato broth

This soup can be made either with bouillon cubes or homemade chicken stock. The latter option will take longer to cook, but it is preferable. However, the smell of fresh chicken stock might be off-putting to some patients.

1 small onion
2 carrots
2 celery stalks
2 ripe tomatoes
1 chicken leg or 2 chicken
   bouillon cubes

1 blade of mace
1 bay leaf
sprig of fresh thyme
salt and pepper

6–8 small portions

Peel and chop the onion and the carrots. Wash and chop the celery, and tomatoes.

Bring $3^{1}/_{2}$ cups water to a boil with the chicken leg or bouillon cubes. While the chicken is cooking, skim the broth. If using cubes, stir until they are dissolved.

Add the vegetables, the spices, the herbs, and a pinch each of salt and pepper. Let it simmer over a low heat. If using bouillon cubes, simmer for 30 minutes; if using the chicken leg, simmer for 2 hours.

Strain the stock, reserving the vegetables, and the chicken, and season to taste.

Serve in small bowls. Some of the cooked vegetables and a few small pieces of the chicken can be added, depending upon how difficult it is for the patient to swallow.

Keep the rest of the soup in the fridge or freezer.

FOR A FAMILY OF FOUR:
SERVE AS AN APPETIZER.

cream of eggplant and tomato soup

When prepared without stock, this recipe can be turned into a lovely puree to be enjoyed on its own or on a slice of soft bread.

¹/₂ slice wholewheat bread
¹/₄ eggplant
1 small tomato
2 scallions
1 garlic clove
3 tablespoons olive oil

pinch of ground cumin
1 cup vegetable stock from
   a stock cube or homemade
salt and pepper

2–3 small portions

Remove the crusts and cut the bread into cubes. Wash and chop the eggplants, tomato, and scallions. Peel and chop the garlic.

Heat the olive oil in a saucepan. Add the eggplant, tomato, scallions, and garlic. Fry for 3 minutes over a medium heat. Add a pinch of ground cumin, the bread, and the stock. Cook until the eggplant is very soft, 10–15 minutes.

Whizz to a very smooth soup in a blender or food-processor. Season to taste.

Pour into small bowls.

Tip: If it appeals to the patient, you could reserve a tablespoon of scallion to sprinkle over the soup just before serving.

FOR A FAMILY OF FOUR:
MULTIPLY THE INGREDIENTS BY FOUR AND SERVE AS AN APPETIZER.

vegetable soup

It's best to make this soup in large quantities and then keep it in the fridge for a few days. It can also be frozen, preferably in small portions, so it is easy to defrost just what you need.

1 small carrot
1/4 leek
1 celery stalk
4 button or shiitake mushrooms
1 tomato

3 sprigs of fresh parsley
1 vegetable bouillon cube
salt and pepper

3–4 small portions

Peel, wash and then cut all the vegetables and herbs very fine (this is easily done in a food-processor).

Bring 1³/₄ cups water to a boil with the bouillon cube and the vegetables. Simmer for 15–30 minutes. The longer they cook, the softer the vegetables will be.

Add salt and pepper to taste.

Serve in small bowls. Keep the rest of the soup in the fridge or freeze it.

Tip: This vegetable soup may also be pureed and all sorts of herbs and spices can be added to taste: try curry powder, paprika, thyme, chives, or dill.

FOR A FAMILY OF FOUR:
DOUBLE THE INGREDIENTS AND SERVE AS AN APPETIZER.

pumpkin soup with soy sauce

Pumpkin has a sweet taste and when cooked it has a very soft texture. It's lovely as a base for soups. It can be replaced by other soft vegetables such as eggplant, sweet potato, zucchini, or asparagus.

1/2 slice wholewheat bread
5-ounce wedge of pumpkin
1 small onion
1 garlic clove
sprig of fresh parsley or cilantro
3 tablespoons olive oil

pinch of curry powder
1 cup chicken stock from a
    stock cube or homemade
splash of soy sauce

2 small portions

Remove the crusts and cut the bread into cubes. Peel and chop the pumpkin, onion and garlic. Chop the parsley or cilantro fine.

Heat the olive oil in a saucepan. Add the pumpkin, the onion, and the garlic. Fry for 3 minutes over a medium heat. Add a pinch of curry powder, the bread, and the stock. Cook until the pumpkin is very soft, about 10–15 minutes.

Whizz to a very smooth soup in a blender or food-processor. Add soy sauce to taste.

Pour into two small bowls and sprinkle with the parsley or cilantro.

Tip: Some spiciness, such as Tabasco, and acidity, such as lemon or lime juice, can be added at the table according to personal taste.

FOR A FAMILY OF FOUR:
MULTIPLY THE INGREDIENTS BY FOUR AND SERVE AS AN APPETIZER.

indian tea with milk and spices

This aromatic tea is normally served hot or warm. However, it is also very nice to serve it chilled.

1 cup lowfat or soy milk
1 bay leaf
2 cardamom seeds
1 tablespoon green tea leaves
honey to taste

2 small portions

Bring the milk to a boil with a scant $1/2$ cup water, the bay leaf, and the cardamom seeds. Let it simmer for 5 minutes.

Turn off the heat. Add the tea leaves and let steep for 5 minutes.

Strain the tea into two glasses or cups. Add honey to taste.

FOR A FAMILY OF FOUR:
MULTIPLY THE INGREDIENTS BY FOUR.

flavorings

Adding herbs and spices is a touchy subject. You will have to find out by trial and error how much salt, pepper, herbs, spices, and honey is enjoyable for the patient. It's much easier to add a few extra flavorings at the table than having to make a dish, which is too strongly flavoured, milder.

hot anise milk

Milk is not always easy to drink, but served warm it often feels good. The milk in this recipe can be replaced by tea.

1 cup lowfat milk or soy milk
$\frac{1}{2}$ teaspoon grated orange zest
2 tablespoons anise seeds
$\frac{1}{2}$–1 tablespoon honey

2 small portions

Heat the milk for 10 minutes with the orange zest, the anise, and honey to taste. Don't let it boil. Whisk well.

Strain the anise milk into two cups or heatproof glasses.

Tip: Only the orange zest is used in this recipe. The rest of the orange can be kept in the fridge for a day or so until needed.

FOR A FAMILY OF FOUR:
MULTIPLY THE INGREDIENTS BY THREE.

very fine food
Pureed foods can always be made finer, by rubbing them carefully through a fine mesh strainer.

honey and pear soup

Sweet fruit soups normally need a little bit of acidity for a proper balance in taste. As people's taste alters so much during treatment, it may be necessary to fine-tune the sour and sweet components.

$\frac{1}{2}$ slice wholewheat bread
1 ripe pear
1 small lemon
$\frac{1}{2}$–1 tablespoon honey
$\frac{1}{2}$ cup whipping or soy cream

2 small portions

Remove the crusts and cut the bread into cubes.

Peel, then core, quarter, and chop it. Wash and zest the lemon. Juice half of the lemon.

Bring $\frac{3}{4}$ of the lemon juice to a boil with the zest, the bread, the pear quarters and honey to taste. Cook for 10 minutes, stirring regularly.

Whizz in a blender or food-processor to a smooth puree. Add the cream. Cook for a minute longer. Add more lemon juice to taste.

Pour into two small bowls.

Tip: As an alternative you could use apple, peach, or mango.

FOR A FAMILY OF FOUR:
MULTIPLY THE INGREDIENTS BY THREE AND SERVE AS A DESSERT.

warm apple juice with cinnamon

For this recipe, it's best to use a juicer. This kitchen tool makes it very easy to prepare fresh fruit and vegetable juices in a matter of minutes.

3 sweet and juicy apples
1 teaspoon honey
1 cinnamon stick

2 small portions

Wash, peel and core the apples. Juice them in a juicer.

Bring the juice to a boil with the honey and cinnamon stick. Let it simmer for 5 minutes, then remove the cinnamon stick. Stir well for 1 minute.

Pour the warm juice into two heatproof glasses or cups.

Tip: If you don't have a juicer, you could use natural apple juice.

FOR A FAMILY OF FOUR:
MULTIPLY THE INGREDIENTS BY FOUR.

chapter five

crispy

mini potato pancakes with egg salad

If you think the taste of scallions will be too strong in this recipe, replace them with fresh chives. These mini pancakes are also very nice with other salads or with smoked fish, shrimp, or thinly sliced meats.

1 egg
2 small scallions
3 sprigs of fresh parsley
1 tablespoon mayonnaise
pinch of salt

pinch of pepper
1 small potato
splash of olive oil

2 small portions

Boil the egg for 8 minutes, then hold it under cold running water and let it cool.

Chop the scallions and parsley. Shell the egg. Chop it and mix it with 3/4 of the spring onion, 3/4 of the parsley, the mayonnaise, and a pinch each of salt and pepper.

Peel the potato and grate it on a fine grater but don't rinse it afterwards. Mix with a pinch each of salt and pepper. Put it in a strainer to drain.

Heat a good splash of oil in a big frying pan. Put 6 small spoonfuls of grated potato beside each other in the pan. Flatten the heaps of potato with the back of the spoon and fry the potato pancakes for a few minutes until golden brown and cooked. Put them on paper towels to absorb any fat.

Place the six potato pancakes on two small plates. Divide the egg salad between the pancakes and sprinkle with the remaining scallions and parsley.

Tip: Half the amount of mayonnaise can be replaced by plain yogurt or sour cream. Mix thoroughly.

FOR A FAMILY OF FOUR:
DOUBLE THE INGREDIENTS AND SERVE AS AN APPETIZER.

vegetable sticks with a walnut dip

If you want to use this dip as a salad dressing, add a little lemon juice. You could also prepare it with pecans, macadamia nuts, or a nut mixture.

6 walnut halves
1 tablespoon mayonnaise
1 tablespoon plain or soy yogurt
pinch of salt
pinch of pepper

2 celery stalks
1/8 cucumber
1/8 red pepper

2 small portions

Chop the walnuts fine. Add the mayonnaise, the yogurt, and the salt and pepper.

Wash the vegetables and deseed the pepper. Cut the vegetables into thin sticks.

Put the walnut dip into small bowls and the vegetable sticks into two small glasses. Put a bowl and a glass of each on two small plates.

FOR A FAMILY OF FOUR:
DOUBLE THE INGREDIENTS AND SERVE AS A SNACK OR AN APPETIZER.

melba toast with smoked salmon and fennel

This is made with raw fennel, which is nice and crispy. If swallowing is difficult, the fennel can be cooked first to soften it. You could also use soft bread instead of toast.

1/4 fennel bulb
1 teaspoon lemon juice
1/2 teaspoon honey
pinch of salt
pinch of pepper
2 tablespoons flaxseed oil
2 small slices smoked salmon (lox)
4 small Melba toasts (preferably
    wholewheat)
1 tablespoon light cream cheese

2 small portions

Slice the fennel very thin. Set aside some of the fronds.

Mix the lemon juice with the honey in a big bowl. Stir until the honey is dissolved. Add the salt and pepper, and the oil. Mix well. Add the fennel and let it stand for at least 15 minutes (a few hours would be even better).

Slice the salmon in half. Spread the Melba toasts with cream cheese.

Place on two small plates. Top with the salmon first and then the fennel salad. Garnish with some fennel fronds.

Tip: Instead of Melba toast, you could also use thinly sliced and toasted wholewheat bread. If dairy products cause problems, you can leave out the cream cheese.

FOR A FAMILY OF FOUR:
THIS WILL BE ENOUGH FOR FOUR PEOPLE TO SERVE AS A SNACK. TO SERVE AS AN APPETIZER, DOUBLE THE INGREDIENTS.

snacks

When buying ready-made snacks, try and go for untreated products without preservatives. Hydrogenated fats can be a problem, especially in crispy snacks, so check the labels first. Recommended ready–to-eat crispy snacks are apples, muesli, radishes, and a selection of nuts, but not peanuts.

tortilla and guacamole chips

This guacamole can also be served as a filling for sandwiches or as a spread on toast. It's nice to add some fresh chives or fresh cilantro.

1 small ripe avocado
1 teaspoon of lemon
   or lime juice
1 small tomato
1 scallion
2 tablespoons sour cream
   or soy yogurt
pinch of salt
pinch of chili powder
3½ ounces tortilla chips

3–4 small portions

Cut the avocado in half and remove the pit. Scoop out the flesh and put it in a bowl. Mash lightly with a fork. Add the juice.

Cut the tomato into small pieces and the scallion into thin rings. Add to the avocado. Fold in the sour cream. Season with a pinch of salt and a pinch of chili powder.

Fill three or four small bowls, put them on small plates, and arrange the tortilla chips around them.

Tip: If you prefer, the tomato can be skinned first. Put it into boiling water for 15 seconds, rinse under cold water, and remove the skin with a knife.

FOR A FAMILY OF FOUR:
THIS WILL BE ENOUGH FOR FOUR PEOPLE TO SERVE AS A SNACK.
TO SERVE AS AN APPETIZER, DOUBLE THE INGREDIENTS.

caesar salad

It's a good idea to use wholewheat bread for the croutons because it is good for the digestive system. However, if white bread really is preferred, it can also be used. The Parmesan cheese is grated but it could also be shaved into thin slivers.

1 slice wholewheat bread
1/4 cup olive oil
1 small lemon
2 sprigs of fresh parsley
3 anchovy fillets
1 tablespoon mayonnaise
1 tablespoon plain or soy yogurt

2 tablespoons grated Parmesan
   cheese
pinch of pepper
8–10 small lettuce
   or Romaine salad leaves

3–4 small portions

Remove the crusts and cut the bread into small cubes. Heat the oil and fry the bread cubes for a few minutes until they are crispy. Spoon them onto a piece of paper towel.

Wash the lemon and grate the zest. Cut the lemon in half and squeeze out the juice. Chop the parsley very fine. Cut 1 anchovy into long strips.

Pound 2 anchovies to a paste with a mortar and pestle (this can also be done with a fork in a small dish). Add 1 teaspoon of lemon zest, half the parsley, the mayonnaise, the yogurt, half of the cheese and a pinch of pepper. Add lemon juice to taste—about 1/2 or 1 teaspoon.

Wash and dry the lettuce. Divide between two small plates and pour over the anchovy dressing. Put the anchovy strips on top of the salad and then add the croutons, the remaining cheese, and the rest of the parsley.

Tip: For a more pungent taste, add a dash of red pepper sauce such as Tabasco.

FOR A FAMILY OF FOUR:
2 SLICES OF BREAD AND FRY THEM IN 1/3 CUP OIL. MULTIPLY THE INGREDIENTS FOR THE DRESSING BY FOUR AND USE A WHOLE HEAD OF LETTUCE.

meringues with blueberries and ice cream

Meringues are very sweet and so they go well with fresh fruit. You can buy ready-made meringues or bake them yourself (see tip).

2 small meringue nests
1/3 cup blueberries
2 scoops ice cream
1 tablespoon blueberry or
    blackberry syrup

2 small portions

Place the meringue nests on two small plates. Fill them with some of the blueberries and ice cream.

Sprinkle the rest of the blueberries and the syrup over the ice cream.

Tip: If you want to make meringues yourself, here's how to do it. Preheat the oven to 225°F. Beat 1 egg white with 2 tablespoons sugar and a pinch of salt until very stiff. Spoon 4 heaps of the mixture onto a cookie sheet lined with foil, shiny side up. With the back of a spoon, press down the middle of each meringue mixture to form hollow "nests." Place in the cool oven and let them dry for 2–3 hours.

FOR A FAMILY OF FOUR:
DOUBLE THE INGREDIENTS AND SERVE AS A DESSERT.

everything tastes different

One of the most difficult things to accept during treatment is the fact that tastes can change completely from what you expect them to be. There is very little you can do about this, other than trying to find out, almost on a daily basis, which tastes suit you best.

green tea granita with honey

Making granita is very easy but it does take time because you have to stir regularly during the freezing. This prevents it from becoming one big icy lump. You can replace the tea with all sorts of juices, and other sweetened liquids such as coffee or chocolate milk may also be used.

1 tablespoon green tea
$1/2$–1 tablespoon honey

2 small portions

Put the green tea in a pot and pour in 1 cup of boiling water. Stir in the honey to dissolve. Let cool.

Pour the tea into a small plastic container and freeze it for 3–4 hours, stirring every 15 minutes.

Divide between two glasses and serve immediately, or seal tightly and place in the freezer for several days.

FOR A FAMILY OF FOUR:
MULTIPLY THE INGREDIENTS BY THREE AND SERVE AS A DESSERT OR REFRESHMENT.

strawberry "carpaccio"

This recipe can be made with any fresh fruit that can be sliced thinly such as melon, peach, pear, or mango.

½ tablespoon mixed nuts
½ tablespoon mixed seeds
   (e.g., sunflower seeds, flaxseeds,
   sesame seeds, pumpkin seeds)
2 small meringues
10 ripe strawberries
2 teaspoons strawberry syrup
6 tiny fresh mint leaves

2 small portions

FOR A FAMILY OF FOUR:
MULTIPLY THE INGREDIENTS BY
THREE AND SERVE AS A DESSERT.

Chop the nuts coarsely. Roast the nuts and the seeds for a few minutes in a dry frying pan until they start to color. Slide them onto a plate to cool.

Crumble the meringues.

Wash, hull and thinly slice the strawberries. Overlap the slices, one on top of the other, on two small plates. Sprinkle with the syrup and chill in the fridge for no longer than half a day.

Sprinkle the nuts, seeds, meringue crumbs, and mint leaves over the strawberries just before eating.

Tips: Meringues can be bought ready-made or homemade. See the instructions for making them on page 130.

lemon curd tartlets

These tartlets can be filled with the patient's favorite jam or marmalade. The pastry cases can also be baked blind and filled afterwards with fresh fruit and/or whipped cream.

1/3 cup plain flour
pinch of salt
2 tablespoons sugar
about 2 tablespoons ice cold butter
3 tablespoons lemon curd

4 small tarts

Preheat the oven to 350°F.

Put the flour and a pinch of salt in a mixing bowl. Add the sugar and rub in the butter until the mixture resembles fine breadcrumbs. This can also be done in a food processor. Add 1 teaspoon of water. Knead lightly, cover, and place in the fridge for 20 minutes.

Divide the pastry into four small balls and roll each of them out on a floured board into thin circles about 3 1/2 inches across. Line four individual, greased, shallow tartlet molds or ovenproof dishes with the pastry. Prick some holes in the bottom with a fork. Fill them with the lemon curd. Bake for 15–20 minutes. Let cool.

Serve in the baking dishes.

Tip: Lemon curd can also be homemade. In the top of a double boiler, mix the grated zest of a lemon with 1/3 cup honey and 1 stick minus 1 tablespoon butter in a double boiler. Let the butter melt and the honey dissolve. Little by little, add the juice of a lemon. Beat 2 eggs and stir slowly into the mixture. Stir until the curd is nice and thick. This may take some time.

try not to get upset

Eating is an emotional thing, especially when it suddenly becomes a major effort. Try not to get upset if the food you used to like so much does not taste nice at all. It depends on the type of cancer, but for most people, once the chemotherapy has finished, taste returns to normal and you will be able to enjoy your food again.

FOR A FAMILY OF FOUR:
DOUBLE THE INGREDIENTS AND SERVE WITH COFFEE OR TEA OR AS A DESSERT WITH ICE CREAM ON THE SIDE.

vegetable tempura with a soy dip

You can make beautiful tempura with jumbo shrimp, fish chunks, tender meat, and chicken. Just dip them in the batter and fry until golden and cooked. Make sure you use extra virgin olive oil for frying the tempura, and don't overheat the oil.

6 small shiitake mushrooms
2 carrots
2 small broccoli florets
1/8 red pepper
1/3 cup wholewheat flour
1 egg

pinch of salt
2 tablespoons ground almonds
olive oil
1/4 cup Japanese soy sauce

2–3 small portions

Wipe the shiitake mushrooms, peel the carrots and wash the other vegetables. Cut the carrots into long sticks. Cut the broccoli florets in half, seed the red pepper and cut into two or three pieces.

Mix the flour lightly with the egg, 1/3 cup cold water, a pinch of salt, and the almonds (a little of the flour may still be seen).

Heat about 11/2 inches of olive oil to 325°F. You can test the temperature with a candy thermometer, or by frying a piece of bread—if it turns golden in about 1 minute, it is ready.

Fry the tempura in two or three portions. Dip the shiitake mushrooms and vegetables one by one into the batter and drop into the hot oil immediately. Fry for 3–4 minutes until golden brown. Let them dry on paper towels.

Serve on small plates, with the soy sauce on the side.

Tip: As a variation on a batter made with flour, you could coat the vegetables with beaten egg and wholewheat breadcrumbs.

FOR A FAMILY OF FOUR:
MULTIPLY THE INGREDIENTS BY FOUR AND SERVE AS AN APPETIZER OR A SIDE DISH WITH GRILLED FISH OR CHICKEN.

grilled cheese and tomato sandwich

Toasted cheese sandwiches can be made with any cheese that melts easily and all sorts of tasty ingredients can be added, for example, grilled vegetables, chopped nuts, and sliced meats without preservatives, such as fresh ham from a butcher, or smoked chicken.

2 small tomatoes
small sprig of fresh parsley
2 slices wholewheat bread
1 tablespoon light cream cheese
1 thin slice cheddar cheese, big
    enough to cover a bread slice
1/2 tablespoon olive oil

2 small portions

Wash and then cut the tomatoes in half. Scoop out the seeds and slice the tomatoes into small strips. Chop the parsley fine.

Remove crusts from the bread. Spread both slices with cream cheese. Divide the tomato strips and the parsley over one slice of bread. Cover with the cheddar cheese. Put the other slice of bread (cream cheese side down) on top. Press down lightly and brush with a little olive oil.

Heat a big frying pan, put the sandwich in the pan, oil side down, and toast until brown. Brush the top with a little oil, turn, and toast until brown. Cut the sandwich into quarters and put them on two small plates.

Tip: Wholewheat bread is recommended but if it causes problems, white bread can be used, too. You don't have to use the cream cheese.

FOR A FAMILY OF FOUR:
MULTIPLY THE INGREDIENTS BY FOUR AND SERVE FOR LUNCH.

mild olive oil
During treatment, it's best to avoid very strong tastes, so choose a mild-tasting olive oil.

veal scallops with a cornflake crust

For extra crispness, these scallops are coated with cornflakes. Panko Japanese breadcrumbs also give a really crispy result. If a softer texture is preferred, use fresh wholewheat breadcrumbs instead. Be sure to use extra virgin olive oil to deep-fry the french fries, and make sure that the oil doesn't overheat.

1/3 cup organic cornflakes
1 small, thin veal scallop
olive oil
pinch of salt
pinch of pepper
1/2 egg, beaten
1/2 teaspoon paprika
1 teaspoon honey
1/2 tablespoon balsamic vinegar
4 ounces frozen french fries
1 ounce salad greens (about 1 cup)

2 small portions

Crumble the cornflakes fine.

Cut the veal scallop into six pieces. Cover them with foil, greased with olive oil. Beat them with a wooden mallet or rolling pin to flatten. Season with a pinch of salt, a pinch of pepper, and the paprika.

Dip the veal in the egg and cover both sides with the cornflake crumbs. Place in the fridge for at least 5 minutes.

Mix the honey with the vinegar and 2 tablespoons of olive oil to make a dressing.

Heat about 4 inches of olive oil in a small, deep pan to about 350°F. Fry the french fries until golden brown. Let them dry on paper towels. Sprinkle with a little salt.

Heat a splash of olive oil in the meantime and fry the scallops for a few minutes until brown on both sides.

Dress the salad greens with the dressing. Divide the salad, the meat, and french fries between two small plates.

Tip: As a vegetarian alternative to veal scallops, you could use eggplant slices instead. Season the eggplant, cover with cornflakes, and fry in the same way as the scallops.

FOR A FAMILY OF FOUR:
4 CUPS CORNFLAKES, 4 VEAL SCALLOPS, 1–2 EGGS, 2 TEASPOONS PAPRIKA, 2 TEASPOONS HONEY, 2 TABLESPOONS BALSAMIC VINEGAR, 1/2 CUP OLIVE OIL FOR THE DRESSING, 2 1/4 POUNDS FROZEN FRENCH FRIES AND PLENTY OF OIL TO DEEP-FRY THEM, 7 OUNCES SALAD LEAVES.

cheese and tomato bread pizza

Instead of sliced bread, you could try using a small amount of ready-made pizza dough—about 1¹/₂ ounces should be enough. Roll out the dough very thinly, cover with the sauce and then the cheese mixture, and bake in a very hot oven—not in a pan.

2 large slices wholewheat bread
2 small scallions
2 cherry tomatoes
1 thick slice mozzarella
¹/₂ teaspoon Italian seasoning
2 tablespoons olive oil

¹/₄ cup any tomato sauce such as ketchup, pasta sauce, or tomato puree

2 small portions

Cut circles out of the bread slices with a biscuit cutter or a wide cup.

Wash and slice the scallions thin. Wash and cut the cherry tomatoes into six wedges and the mozzarella into cubes. Mix the mozzarella with the spring onions, tomatoes, and herbs.

Heat the oil in a big frying pan. Fry the bread circles over a low heat until light brown on one side. Turn and spread the tomato sauce over them. Spoon the mozzarella mixture on top. Partially cover the pan. Fry until the other side of the bread is brown and the mozzarella has almost melted.

Serve on two small plates.

Tip: Mozzarella can be replaced by another cheese if you prefer, such as Brie, Camembert, or a blue cheese variety.

FOR A FAMILY OF FOUR:
MULTIPLY THE INGREDIENTS BY FOUR AND SERVE AS AN APPETIZER.

spring rolls with chicken and ginger

These can be prepared in advance. Unfried, they will keep in the fridge for 2 days or even longer in the freezer. Serve the spring rolls with a sweet and sour sauce on the side.

about 4-inch piece of leek
2 small carrots
a marble-sized piece fresh ginger
about 3 tablespoons smoked or
    cooked chicken
1 garlic clove
1–2 tablespoons olive oil

$^1/_2$ tablespoon thick sweet
    soy sauce
1 teaspoon lemon juice
2 thin spring roll sheets (about
    7 inches x 7 inches)

2 small portions

Preheat the oven to 425°F.

Wash the leek. Peel the carrots and ginger. Cut the leek, carrots, ginger, and chicken into long, thin strips. Peel and chop the garlic.

Heat 1 tablespoon of olive oil and fry the vegetables and ginger for 4 minutes over a medium heat. Add the chicken, soy sauce, and lemon juice, and cook for 1 minute more.

Spread out the two spring roll sheets on a counter and brush them with olive oil.

Divide the vegetable mixture into two portions, putting them at the bottom on top of each spring roll sheet, leaving an inch free on each side. Fold the sides over the vegetables and roll from the bottom upwards, quite tightly, so you get a small package.

Brush with a little oil and place them on a small baking tray. Bake in the oven for 10–15 minutes until crispy and brown.

Serve them on two small plates.

FOR A FAMILY OF FOUR:
MULTIPLY THE INGREDIENTS BY FOUR AND SERVE AS AN APPETIZER.

cherry crumble

Crumbles are easy to make, even in small portions. Any kind of fruit or fruit compote can also be used.

2 tablespoons wholewheat flour
pinch of salt
1 tablespoon cold butter
1$\frac{1}{2}$ tablespoons confectioners' sugar
pinch of cinnamon
3$\frac{1}{2}$ ounces cherries (fresh, frozen,
  or from a jar)
2 tablespoons cherry jam, preferably
  100% fruit, with no sugar added

2–3 small portions

Preheat the oven to 400°F.

Put the flour and a pinch of salt in a mixing bowl. Rub in the butter until the mixture resembles fine breadcrumbs. This can also be done in a food processor. Stir in the confectioners' sugar and cinnamon and mix well. Keep in the fridge until ready to use.

Pit the cherries, if necessary. Mix the cherries with the jam.

Divide the cherry mixture between two or three greased ramekins or other individual ovenproof dishes. Spoon the crumble mixture over the top.

Bake for about 20 minutes, until the crumble is golden and crispy. Serve hot.

Tip: This may be served with whipped cream or ice cream on the side.

FOR A FAMILY OF FOUR:
MULTIPLY THE INGREDIENTS BY FOUR AND SERVE AS A DESSERT.

a preference for sweet or savory

Most people express a definite preference for either sweet or savory dishes. During treatment, the idea of a normal menu progression from savory to sweet no longer applies. The sweet dishes in this book are therefore definitely not meant as desserts, but rather as an alternative to savory dishes. Two dishes are often simply too much to eat at one sitting.

bread and butter pudding with hazelnuts

This easy-to-prepare bread pudding can be made with any type of bread and even with cake. It doesn't matter if the slices are a wee bit stale. Instead of using butter, you can sprinkle the bread with a mild olive oil.

1 tablespoon raisins
1 tablespoon unsalted roasted
  hazelnuts
1 1/2 slices wholewheat bread,
  cut in half diagonally
1 tablespoon soft butter

1 egg
1/2–1 tablespoon honey
1/4 cup whipping or soy cream
1/2 tablespoon sugar

2 small portions

Soak the raisins for 15 minutes in warm water, drain and leave to dry.

Preheat the oven to 350°F.

Chop the hazelnuts coarsely and mix with the raisins. Remove the crusts and cut each bread slice diagonally in half again to make six triangles. Butter them on both sides.

Beat the egg with the honey and cream until dissolved.

Place a bread triangle at an angle at the bottom of two dishes, top with 1/4 of the raisin and hazelnut mixture, then with another triangle. Layer with another 1/4 of the raisin and hazelnut mixture and finish with a bread triangle. Pour the egg mixture over them and soak for 3 minutes.

Sprinkle with sugar and bake in the oven for about 20 minutes until brown and crispy. Serve warm.

Tip: Bread and butter pudding can be served on its own or with whipped cream or custard.

FOR A FAMILY OF FOUR:
MULTIPLY THE INGREDIENTS BY THREE AND SERVE AS A DESSERT.

grilled apple sandwich

This type of sandwich can be toasted in a frying pan on in a special iron griddle that you hold over the burner on your stove.

½ apple
4 slices wholewheat bread
½ tablespoon soft butter
1 teaspoon honey
½ teaspoon cinnamon

2 small portions

Peel and core the apple half. Cut into very thin slices.

Cut a big circle out of each slice of bread using a bowl or biscuit cutter. Spread the bread circles thinly with butter. Cover two with slices of apple and sprinkle with honey and cinnamon. Place the other circles of bread on top (butter side down). Press it down a little. Butter the top lightly.

Heat a frying pan. Put the sandwich, butter side down, in the pan and fry until brown. Butter the top and turn the sandwich to fry the other side.

Cut the sandwiches in half and serve on two small plates.

Tip: You could replace the apple with banana slices and then you don't have to use butter.

FOR A FAMILY OF FOUR:
MULTIPLY THE INGREDIENTS BY FOUR
AND SERVE AS A SNACK.

orange crème brûlée

The perfect moment to serve the crème brûlée is when the caramel on the top has turned crispy. It is easiest to prepare this dessert a day in advance and then to caramelize the sugar under the broiler shortly before serving. As sugar is not really recommended, it is best to eat this sort of dish only on special occasions. You can broil the crème without the sugar. It will turn a lovely brown but it won't be crispy.

1 small orange
1/2 cup whipping or soy cream
1 egg yolk
2 teaspoons instant vanilla pudding
2 tablespoons honey
about 2 tablespoons sugar

2–3 small portions

Wash the orange and grate half into a small saucepan. Cut the orange in half and squeeze it. Pour the juice into the saucepan. Boil it until it's reduced to 2 tablespoons of juice. Add the cream and return to a boil.

Beat the egg yolk with the instant pudding and the honey for about 5 minutes until light and creamy.

Pour in the hot orange cream in a thin stream, stirring constantly. Pour the mixture back into the saucepan and let it simmer for a few minutes over a very low heat. Keep stirring.

Fill two or three small individual oven dishes with the crème. Let them cool and keep them in the fridge until needed.

Preheat a broiler or oven to the highest temperature.

Sprinkle the crème with the sugar. Place the dishes under a broiler or in the oven and let the sugar caramelize and turn brown.

Tip: If the ovenproof dishes you're using are very wide across, use extra sugar to get an even, crispy layer.

FOR A FAMILY OF FOUR:
MULTIPLY THE INGREDIENTS BY FOUR AND SERVE AS A DESSERT.

too sharp for comfort

Foods that are normally tasty and delicious for healthy people might not be quite so enjoyable for those who are undergoing treatment. For example, pure orange juice could have a nasty sour and sharp taste. However, you will find out that cooking causes the sharpness to disappear and you can also mix it with honey or banana to soften the taste.

chapter six

firm

creamed chicken sandwich

You may want to warm the bread before making this sandwich. This is easily done in a hot oven—just pop it in for a few minutes.

about 3 tablespoons cooked chicken
1 small, sweet, pickled gherkin
1 tablespoon mayonnaise
pinch of salt
pinch of pepper
1 small French crusty roll
4 small lettuce leaves
1 tablespoon cranberry sauce

2 small portions

Whizz the chicken, gherkin, and 2 tablespoons of the liquid from the gherkin jar to a fine cream in a blender or food processor. Add the mayonnaise and season with a pinch of salt and pepper.

Cut the roll into four long diagonal slices. Spread each slice with a quarter of the creamed chicken. Wash and dry the lettuce leaves and then place a lettuce leaf on each of the slices. Top each with the cranberry sauce.

Serve on two small plates.

FOR A FAMILY OF FOUR:
MULTIPLY THE INGREDIENTS FOR THE CREAMED CHICKEN BY FOUR, USE 4 SMALL CRUSTY ROLLS, 16 LETTUCE LEAVES, 2–3 TABLESPOONS OF CRANBERRY SAUCE. SERVE AS A LIGHT LUNCH.

rye bread with cottage cheese and grapes

Rye bread has a coarse texture that can be very pleasant. However, it might not be so appropriate for people who have difficulty swallowing. In this case, replace the rye bread with soft bread, preferably wholewheat.

sprig of fresh parsley
sprig of fresh mint
1 small bunch seedless grapes
2 slices dark rye bread
1/3 cup cottage cheese

pinch of salt
pinch of pepper
pinch of paprika

2 small portions

Remove the parsley and mint leaves from their stalks. Set aside a couple of leaves of each herb and chop the rest fine. Wash the grapes and cut in half.

Place the slices of rye bread on two small plates. Spoon the cottage cheese on top.

Divide the grapes between the two cottage cheese-covered pieces of bread. Sprinkle with a pinch of salt, a pinch each of pepper and paprika, and with the herbs. Place the reserved herb leaves on top.

Tip: As an alternative to grapes, strawberries or slices of apple may be used.

FOR A FAMILY OF FOUR:
DOUBLE THE INGREDIENTS AND SERVE AS A SNACK.

grilled vegetable and mozzarella salad

With its soft and sweetish taste, balsamic vinegar should appeal to patients. However, for some people it might still taste acidic, in which case, mix it with some honey.

sprig of fresh basil
1/8 yellow pepper
1/4 zucchini
1/4 fennel bulb
3 cherry tomatoes
1/2 tablespoon olive oil
pinch of salt
pinch of pepper
1/2 tablespoon balsamic vinegar
1/2 ball of mozzarella or 3 mini balls
6 small lettuce leaves

2 small portions

Remove the basil leaves from the stem and set aside for the garnish. Finely chop the stem.

Wash the vegetables. Cut the pepper in half and seed it. Slice the zucchini and fennel. Cut the cherry tomatoes in half. Brush each of the vegetables with a little olive oil and grill them in a grill pan or under a broiler for a few minutes on each side.

Sprinkle the warm vegetables with 1/2 tablespoon of olive oil, a pinch each of salt and pepper, the chopped basil stems and 1/4 tablespoon of balsamic vinegar. Set aside to cool.

Cut the mozzarella into wedges. Wash and dry the lettuce leaves and arrange them on two small plates. Scatter the grilled vegetables, mozzarella wedges, and basil leaves over them.

Tip: The mozzarella can be replaced by a stronger tasting cheese, like Gorgonzola.

FOR A FAMILY OF FOUR:
MULTIPLY THE INGREDIENTS BY FOUR AND SERVE AS AN APPETIZER.

bigger portions

For most patients, small portions work best during treatment. However, should a patient ask for more, you can easily just prepare bigger portions.

apple, celery, and brazil nut quiche

Quiches like this are great to have on hand. Properly covered and kept in the fridge, they will last for about 3 days. They may also be served warm. If you wish, you can make this without cheese.

2 eggs
1/4 cup flour
pinch of salt
2 tablespoons cold butter
1 small celery stalk
1 scallion
2 brazil nuts

1 small, thin slice of bacon
1 tablespoon olive oil
pinch of pepper
2 tablespoons grated cheddar
  cheese

2 small portions

Separate one of the eggs. Beat the yolk.

Put the flour and a pinch of salt in a mixing bowl and rub in the butter until the mixture resembles fine breadcrumbs. This can also be done in a food-processor. Stir in 1 tablespoon of the beaten egg yolk and 1 teaspoon of cold water. Knead lightly, cover, and chill in the fridge for 20 minutes.

Preheat the oven to 350°F.

Wash the celery and scallion and chop fine. Chop the Brazil nuts fine. Slice the bacon fine.

Heat the oil in a pan and fry the bacon with the celery for 5 minutes. Add the spring onion and fry for 2 minutes. Stir in the nuts.

Add the egg white and the other whole egg to the rest of the yolk. Beat well and season.

Divide the pastry into two small balls and roll them out on a floured surface to 4 inches. Line two small ovenproof dishes with the pastry. Prick the pastry with a fork. Fill the dishes with the celery mixture, sprinkle with the cheese, and pour in the eggs.

Bake for 20–25 minutes in the oven. Set aside to cool. Serve cold or warm.

Tip: Brazil nuts contain vitamin E and enhance the effects of selenium (an antioxidant).

FOR A FAMILY OF FOUR:
DOUBLE THE INGREDIENTS AND SERVE AS AN APPETIZER.

sweet and sour shrimp

This also tastes good with a few tablespoons of pineapple or mango pieces. Stir them in with the scallions.

about ¹/₂ cup instant brown rice
2 small broccoli florets
2 scallions
1 garlic clove
2 raw jumbo shrimp
1 tablespoon olive oil

1–2 teaspoons lime juice
¹/₄ cup tomato ketchup
1 teaspoon thick sweet
  soy sauce

2 small portions

Cook the rice in boiling water following the instructions on the package. Drain.

Wash the broccoli and scallions. Cut the broccoli into very small florets. Slice the scallions. Peel and chop the garlic.

Peel the shrimp but leave the tails on. Cut them lengthwise in the direction of the tail but don't cut all the way through. Remove the black/brown intestine.

Heat the oil in a wok or frying pan and stir-fry the broccoli for 3 minutes. Add the shrimp and stir-fry for another 3 minutes. Add the scallions and garlic and, after 1 minute, stir in the lime juice to taste, and the tomato ketchup and soy sauce.

Divide the rice and sweet and sour shrimp between two small plates. Serve cold or warm.

Tip: You can also add some hot pepper sauce such as Tabasco for a bit of pep.

FOR A FAMILY OF FOUR:
1³/₄ CUPS INSTANT BROWN RICE, 1¹/₄ POUNDS BROCCOLI, A LARGE BUNCH OF SCALLIONS, 3 GARLIC CLOVES, 18 OUNCES RAW SHRIMP, A SPLASH OF OLIVE OIL, THE JUICE OF 1 SMALL LIME, ²/₃ CUP KETCHUP, 1–2 TABLESPOONS OF THICK SWEET SOY SAUCE. SERVE AS A MAIN COURSE.

individual apple pies

Apple is a much-loved fruit and readily available. It also works well with other ingredients such as nuts, raisins, and currants, which can be added according to taste.

1/3 cup wholewheat flour
pinch of salt
2 tablespoons sugar
2 1/2 tablespoons ice-cold butter
1 small lemon
1 small apple or 1/2 apple
1 teaspoon honey
1/2 teaspoon cinnamon
1 tablespoon lowfat or soy milk

2 small pies

Put the flour and a pinch of salt in a mixing bowl, add the sugar, and rub in the butter until the mixture resembles fine breadcrumbs. This can also be done in a food-processor. Add 1 teaspoon of water. Knead lightly, form into a ball, and wrap in waxed paper or plastic wrap. Chill in the fridge for 20 minutes.

Preheat the oven to 350°F.

Wash the lemon and grate a quarter of the zest. Cut in half and squeeze out the lemon juice. Peel and core the apple. Cut into wedges and then cut the wedges into slices. Mix them with the lemon zest, 2 teaspoons of lemon juice, the honey, and cinnamon.

Divide the pastry into four small balls and roll each of them out on a floured surface into thin 3 1/4-inch circles. Line two individual ovenproof dishes or pie plates with a circle of dough each. Prick the pastry with a fork and fill the dishes with the apple slices.

Cover the apple filing with the remaining pastry circles and crimp the two layers together with a thumb and index finger. Make a hole in the middle.

Bake for 20–25 minutes in the hot oven. Brush the top with some milk and bake for a few minutes longer. Set aside to cool.

Tip: Brushing the tops of the apple pies with a few drops of milk gives a nice shine to the pastry. You could also use beaten egg, which should be brushed on at the start, before the pies are first put into the oven.

FOR A FAMILY OF FOUR:
DOUBLE THE INGREDIENTS AND SERVE AS A SNACK WITH A CUP OF COFFEE OR TEA, OR WITH ICE CREAM AS A DESSERT.

snacks

Some good ready-to-eat firm snacks are quiches, mini pizzas, pears, and pineapple. Try and stay away from E numbers and hydrogenated fats—always check the labels.

apricot and pine nut yogurt roll

Fresh apricots are very good in this recipe but, since they are not always available, dried fruit is used. If you use fresh apricots, cut them in half, remove the pit, and chop and mix them into the dough.

¹/₃ cup plain or soy yogurt	¹/₄ cup pine nuts
1 small tablespoon olive oil	6 ready-to-eat dried apricots
¹/₃ cup wholewheat flour	¹/₂ teaspoon confectioners' sugar
pinch of salt	
2 tablespoons honey	**2–3 small portions**

Mix the yogurt with the olive oil, flour, salt, and 1 tablespoon of honey. Work it quickly to a soft dough. Place in the fridge to rest for 20 minutes.

Dry-fry the pine nuts in a dry frying pan until light brown and set them aside to cool on a plate.

Preheat the oven to 350°F.

Cut the apricots into small pieces.

Roll out the dough on a floured surface into a thick 5 x 5-inch square. Sprinkle the apricots and pine nuts on top and push into the dough. Drizzle the rest of the honey over it.

Roll up the dough and cut it into six slices. Grease a baking tray or line it with baking parchment and place the slices on it to bake for about 30 minutes or until golden brown. Set aside to cool.

Place the rolls on two or three small plates and dust with confectioners' sugar.

Tip: The pine nuts can be replaced by macadamias, pecans, or cashews, all chopped coarsely.

FOR A FAMILY OF FOUR:
DOUBLE THE INGREDIENTS AND SERVE WITH A CUP OF COFFEE OR TEA.

fresh fruit popsicles

These popsicles can be made with all sorts of individual soft fruits or a mixture. Hard fruits like apples and pears can also be used but have to be peeled and cooked first in a small pan with a few spoonfuls of water until soft. The popsicles can be kept in the freezer for weeks.

2 cups mixed strawberries,
   raspberries, and cherries
2–4 tablespoons honey
1 tablespoon lemon juice

serves 3–6

Wash the strawberries, raspberries, and cherries, then pit the cherries.

Whizz all the fruit in a blender or food processor, with honey to taste, and the lemon juice.

Fill 3–6 popsicle molds with the fruit mixture so they are three quarters full. Place the sticks in the molds and let freeze in the freezer for a few hours.

Take the fresh fruit popsicles out of the molds just before you are going to eat them.

Tip: The size and number of the popsicles depends on the size of the popsicle molds.

FOR A FAMILY OF FOUR:
THE RECIPE IS ENOUGH FOR A FAMILY IF YOU ARE USING SMALL MOLDS. IF THE FRUIT MIXTURE DOESN'T FILL UP ENOUGH MOLDS, DOUBLE THE INGREDIENTS.

fruit and nougat cups

These cakes are easy to make and can be filled with all sorts of tasty ingredients like caramels, nuts, pieces of chocolate, and berries. In this recipe, nougat and dried fruits are used as the filling.

3 pieces (about 1 ounce) soft nougat
1 piece (about 1 ounce) dried mango
  or 2 dried apricots
1/3 cup wholewheat flour
1 teaspoon baking powder
pinch of salt
3 tablespoons butter
3 tablespoons beaten egg
2 1/2 tablespoons honey
about 3 tablespoons lowfat or soy milk

serves 3–4

Preheat the oven to 425°F.

Cut the nougat and dried mango or apricots into small pieces.

Mix the flour with the baking powder and a pinch of salt. Add the nougat, mango and apricot pieces.

Melt the butter. Mix the egg with the honey and the milk and stir into the butter. Beat the milk mixture quickly into the flour mixture.

Fill three or four small greased ramekins or ovenproof cups with the batter. Bake in the oven for 10 minutes, then turn down the heat down to 350°F. Bake for another 5–10 minutes or until golden brown. Let cool, and serve in the ramekins.

Tip: Honey can be used instead of sugar as it is thought to be healthier than sugar. However, it won't give the cakes as good a texture.

FOR A FAMILY OF FOUR:
DOUBLE THE INGREDIENTS AND SERVE WITH A CUP OF COFFEE OR TEA.

problems with dairy

If eating or drinking dairy products results in heightened mucus production, you'd better choose savory dishes using dairy products as the salt in savory foods has a clearing effect on the mucus.

grilled chicken with fried potatoes

These chicken skewers are very tasty as they are but are also good
served with a small portion of apple sauce or cranberry sauce.

1 small red onion
2 sprigs of fresh mint
2 small potatoes
3 ounces chicken breast
1¹/₂ tablespoons olive oil

pinch of salt
pinch of pepper
¹/₃ cup fresh or frozen peas

2 small portions

Peel the onion and cut into four wedges. Cut the wedges in half
and take the layers of onion apart. Remove the leaves from the
mint sprigs. Leave the small leaves whole and cut the bigger
ones in half. Peel the potatoes and slice thinly.

Cut the chicken into 12 small cubes. Mix them with 1 teaspoon
of olive oil and a pinch each of salt and pepper.

Skewer pieces of chicken, onion, and mint leaves onto six small
skewers. Chop the rest of the onion and mint fine, and set aside
in separate piles.

Cook the peas in boiling water until quite soft. Drain and mix
with the chopped mint.

Heat 1 tablespoon of oil in a frying pan. Lay the potato slices
in the pan and fry until golden brown on both sides, turning
them every so often. Add the chopped onion and fry lightly.

Grill the chicken skewers in a hot grill pan or under the broiler
until brown and well done.

Arrange the potatoes, peas, and skewers on two small plates.

Tip: The chicken skewers (prepared but uncooked) can be kept
in the fridge for a day.

FOR A FAMILY OF FOUR:
3 SMALL RED ONIONS, A SMALL BUNCH OF FRESH MINT, 2¹/₄ POUNDS
POTATOES, 11 OUNCES CHICKEN, ¹/₄ CUP OLIVE OIL, 1¹/₄ POUNDS PEAS.

baked potatoes with spinach cream and ham

The baked potatoes are cut open and slightly scruffed up before serving, and the cream is put on top. If a finer texture is preferred, the potato flesh can be scooped out, pureed with the spinach cream, and then spooned back into the skin for an appetizing look.

2 small baking potatoes
pinch of salt
1 thin slice fresh ham without
   preservatives, from the butcher
1 small onion
3¹/₂ ounces spinach

¹/₂ tablespoon olive oil
2 tablespoons crème fraîche
  or soy yogurt
pinch of pepper

2 small portions

Preheat the oven to 425°F.

Scrub the potatoes under running water and place each on a piece of foil. Sprinkle with the salt and fold the foil tightly around the potatoes. Put them on a baking tray and bake for about 1 hour or until done.

Cut the ham into small ribbons. Peel and chop the onion. Wash, dry, and chop the spinach.

Heat the oil in a frying pan and fry the onion for 3 minutes over a low heat. Raise the heat, add the spinach, and stir-fry for 4 minutes. Strain the mixture until most of the liquid has been removed.

Mix in the ham and the crème fraîche just before serving. Season with a pinch of salt and pepper, and heat for a few minutes.

Remove the potatoes from the oven. Unfold the foil, cut the potatoes open, and criss-cross the potato surface with a fork.

Put the potatoes on small plates and spoon in the spinach cream.

Tip: You can also use frozen spinach or replace it with watercress, arugula, or peas.

FOR A FAMILY OF FOUR:
DOUBLE THE INGREDIENTS AND SERVE AS A STARTER OR SIDE DISH.

baked tortillas

These tortillas can be prepared in advance and kept in the fridge until needed.
Heat them up in the oven just before serving. You don't have to use the cheese.

1/4 red pepper
sprig of fresh cilantro
1 tablespoon olive oil
1/4 cup ground beef or chicken
1/2 teaspoon Mexican or taco spices
2 tablespoons cooked canned
    kidney beans
2 tablespoons canned corn
1/3 cup tomato ketchup or pasta sauce
1 small soft tortilla
1/4 cup grated cheddar cheese
2 tablespoons sour cream or
    soy yogurt

2 small portions

Preheat the oven to 400°F.

Wash, seed, and chop the red pepper. Chop the cilantro.

Heat the olive oil in a big frying pan or wok. Stir-fry the beef or chicken for
3 minutes. Add the red pepper and stir-fry for another 3 minutes. Stir in the
spices, beans, corn, and tomato ketchup or sauce. Simmer for 2 minutes.

Cut the tortilla in half. Fold in the sides to form a cone and put them in one or
two small ovenproof dishes, folded side underneath. Spoon in the bean mixture.
Sprinkle the tortillas with cheese and cover with foil.

Bake for 5 minutes in the oven until nice and warm and the cheese has melted.

Sprinkle with the cilantro and serve in the dish or on small plates. Add sour
cream to taste.

Tip: If it is difficult to get ground chicken, chop chicken meat fine with a sharp
knife, or pulse it in a food processor.

FOR A FAMILY OF FOUR:
2 RED PEPPERS, 6 SPRIGS OF FRESH CILANTRO, 3 TABLESPOONS OLIVE OIL, 7 OUNCES GROUND BEEF
OR CHICKEN, 2 TEASPOONS MEXICAN OR TACO SPICES, 1 x 15-OUNCE CAN KIDNEY BEANS, 1 LARGE
CAN CORN, 1 CUP TOMATO KETCHUP OR SAUCE, 7–8 SMALL SOFT TORTILLAS, 1²/3 CUPS GRATED
CHEDDAR CHEESE, SCANT CUP SOUR CREAM.

the smell of food

For patients, the smell of food often
causes nausea, so naturally it's best
to choose ingredients without a
strong smell. Ideally, try to prepare
food when the patient is not around.
You may even consider using your
neighbour's kitchen. In almost all
cases, it is easier for patients not to
have to cook for themselves.

curried veal stew with pasta

1 small onion
1/2 cup lean stewing veal
pinch of salt
pinch of pepper
1 tablespoon olive oil
1/2 tablespoon mild curry
   powder

3 tablespoons sweet
   white wine
200ml veal stock
2 small nests pappardelle
1/3–1/2 cup fresh or frozen peas
2 tablespoons crème fraîche
   or soy cream

2–3 small portions

Peel and chop the onion. Cut the meat into small cubes of about 5/8 inch and season with the salt and pepper.

Heat the oil in a small frying pan and sauté the meat cubes over a medium heat for a few minutes until brown. Add the onion, sprinkle with the curry powder, and fry for two minutes. Add the wine and the stock. Bring to a boil and then reduce the heat to the very lowest level. Cover and stew for 1 hour until the meat is soft.

Cook the pappardelle in boiling water with a pinch of salt for 2 minutes longer than the instructions on the package. Add the peas 8 minutes before the end of the cooking time. Strain.

Add the crème fraîche or cream to the stew, stir a little, and let it simmer for a few minutes longer. Season.

Divide the pasta and stew between two or three small plates or bowls.

Tip: You can use apple juice instead of wine.

FOR A FAMILY OF FOUR:
MULTIPLY THE INGREDIENTS BY THREE BUT USE **12** OUNCES PAPPARDELLE AND **1**1/4 POUNDS PEAS.

mini meatballs in fresh tomato sauce

Although this recipe uses fresh tomato sauce, you can use ready-made tomato sauce to make life a little easier.

2 potatoes
salt and pepper
sprig of fresh basil
1/4 slice wholewheat bread
1/2 cup finely ground veal or beef
1 1/2 tablespoons beaten egg
1 tablespoon olive oil
2 celery stalks
1 small onion
2 tomatoes

2 small portions

Peel the potatoes and cut them into pieces. Cook in a small pan with a little water and a pinch of salt for 15–20 minutes until they are done. Drain.

Strip the leaves from the basil stalk and reserve. Finely chop the stalk and set aside.

Whizz the bread with half the chopped basil stalk in a blender or food-processor to make breadcrumbs. Mix the ground meat with half of the breadcrumb mixture, a pinch each of salt and pepper, and 1 tablespoon of the beaten egg. Divide into six portions and roll them into balls.

Heat 1/2 tablespoon of oil in a small frying pan and fry the meatballs for about 10 minutes until brown.

Wash the celery stalks. Slice 1 stalks into thin strips. Cut the remaining half-stalk finely into very small pieces. Put the celery strips in a pan of slightly salted boiling water and cook for about 10 minutes. Drain.

Peel and chop the onion. Wash the tomatoes and chop.

Heat 1/2 tablespoon of oil in a frying pan. Add the onion, finely cut celery, and remaining basil stalk. Fry for 3 minutes over a medium heat. Add the tomatoes and a pinch each of salt and pepper, and fry for 2 more minutes. Add 1/3 cup water, the rest of the bread mixture, and the meatballs. Let the sauce simmer for 5 minutes. Adjust the seasoning.

Mash the potatoes in the pan. Return them to the heat and stir in the rest of the egg. Heat for a few minutes and add salt and pepper to taste.

Divide the potato, celery, and mini meatballs with sauce between two small plates. Tear the reserved basil leaves and scatter them over the top.

Tip: Celery works well as an ingredient in the sauce but it's also good as a side dish. It can be replaced by fennel if you wish.

FOR A FAMILY OF FOUR:
2 1/4 POUNDS POTATOES, 1 SLICE WHOLEWHEAT BREAD, 3 SPRIGS OF FRESH BASIL, 1 1/3 CUPS GROUND MEAT, 1 EGG, 1 BUNCH OF CELERY, 2 ONIONS, 4 TOMATOES, 3–4 TABLESPOONS OLIVE OIL. USE THREE QUARTERS OF THE EGG FOR THE MEATBALLS AND THE REST FOR THE POTATOES. USE 1 CELERY STALK FOR THE SAUCE.

fried pineapple

Fresh or canned pineapple can be used in this recipe. Since canned pineapple has already been sweetened, no honey is needed.

1/2 tablespoon shelled sunflower
    seeds
1 slice fresh or canned pineapple
a small pat of butter or a splash
    of olive oil
1/2 tablespoon honey (optional)
2 scoops vanilla ice cream

2 small portions

Dry-fry the sunflower seeds for a few minutes in a dry frying pan over a high heat, stirring all the time. Tip onto a plate to cool.

Cut the pineapple horizontally into two thin slices.

Melt the butter in a frying pan and fry the pineapple for 2 minutes on each side over a medium heat. When fresh pineapple is used, add the honey and let it melt.

Place the pineapple on two small plates. Put a scoop of ice cream in the middle and sprinkle with the sunflower seeds.

Tip: Slices of peeled apple can be prepared in more or less the same way as the pineapple.

FOR A FAMILY OF FOUR:
MULTIPLY THE INGREDIENTS BY FOUR AND SERVE AS A DESSERT.

peanuts are off the menu
Seeds are very good for you and most nuts, too. When using mixed nuts in recipes, choose a selection without peanuts as peanuts aren't recommended for cancer patients.

apple fritters

Fritters often go down well. Try also using bananas, apricots, and pineapple. However, the fruit you choose shouldn't be too juicy (this would make the fritters soggy) and it should have a firm texture.

1 apple
1 tablespoon blanched
  almonds
3 tablespoons wholewheat flour
1/2 beaten egg
pinch of salt

mild olive oil
2 scoops apple or lemon
  sherbet
1 teaspoon confectioners' sugar

2 small portions

Peel and core the apples. Cut into six wedges. Chop the almonds coarsely.

Mix the flour lightly with the egg, 1/3 cup cold water, a pinch of salt, and the almonds.

Heat a layer of about 11/2 inches of olive oil in a saucepan to 325°F. You can test the temperature with a cooking thermometer or by frying a piece of bread, which will turn golden in about 1 minute if the oil is at the right temperature.

Dip the apple wedges one by one into the batter and immediately put them into the hot oil. Fry for 3–4 minutes until golden brown. Remove from the oil and let drain on a piece of paper towel.

Place the scoops of apple or lemon sherbet on two or three small plates. Place the fritters next to them and dust with confectioners' sugar.

Tip: Apple sorbet is not always easy to find. It can be replaced by any other type of sherbet or ordinary ice cream.

FOR A FAMILY OF FOUR:
MULTIPLY THE INGREDIENTS BY FOUR AND SERVE AS A DESSERT.

rice pudding

scant cup lowfat or soy milk
1/3 cup whipping or soy cream
2 tablespoons instant
  short-grain rice
1/2–1 tablespoon honey
3 tablespoons thick berry juice
2 stalks of red currants (optional)

2 small portions

FOR A FAMILY OF FOUR:
MULTIPLY THE INGREDIENTS BY FOUR
AND SERVE AS A DESSERT.

This rice pudding is also nice when served cold. It will get thicker when it cools down and may be made smoother by adding a little more milk or cream. Hot or cold, it tastes good with a tablespoon of chopped nuts.

Bring the milk, cream, rice, and honey to a boil in a small saucepan. Turn down the heat as low as possible and let the mixture simmer until the rice is soft and creamy, stirring every now and then (the cooking time varies per brand so check the package. Clean the red currants, if using, and set aside.

Divide between two small bowls. Pour over the berry juice over them and serve hot. Put the red currants on the side, if using.

Tip: If berry juice is not available, 100% fruit jam can be used.

french toast with red fruit

French toast can also be served with fruit salad made from seasonal fruit.

1/4 cup mixed fresh or frozen
   red fruit such as berries
   and cherries
1 teaspoon honey
1 egg
1 1/2 teaspoons vanilla sugar
pinch of salt
1 slice light wholewheat bread
a small pat of butter or a splash
   of olive oil

2 small portions

Clean the fruit or let it defrost. Mix the fruit with the honey.

Beat the egg with 1 teaspoon of the vanilla sugar and the salt until the sugar has dissolved.

Cut the slice of bread diagonally into four pieces.

Melt the butter or heat the oil in a small frying pan. Dip the pieces of bread deep into the egg mixture and fry them until brown on both sides.

Place the French toast on two small plates. Spoon the fruit over it and dust with the remaining vanilla sugar.

Tip: French toast is usually sweet but it can also be savoury. No sugar is used and chopped fresh herbs and pepper are added to the egg mix. When almost done, grated cheese that melts easily can be sprinkled on top.

FOR A FAMILY OF FOUR:
MULTIPLY THE INGREDIENTS BY FOUR BUT USE ONLY 2 EGGS. SERVE AS A BREAKFAST TREAT.

sharing meals
Patients often find it easier to eat with some company but be aware that they can easily lose their appetite when they see the size of normal portions on other plates.

index